old orchard farm

A BUR OAK BOOK

old orchard farm

THE STORY OF AN IOWA BOYHOOD

by Hugh Orchard

edited by Paul F. Sharp

illustrated by John Huseby

University of Iowa Press, Iowa City

University of Iowa Press, Iowa City 52242
Copyright © 1952 by the Iowa State College Press
University of Iowa Press edition published 2010
www.uiowapress.org
Printed in the United States of America

The University of Iowa Press is a member of Green
Press Initiative and is committed to preserving natural
resources.

Printed on acid-free paper

Library of Congress Cataloging-in-Publication Data
Orchard, Hugh, 1868–1964.
Old Orchard farm: the story of an Iowa boyhood /
Hugh Orchard.—University of Iowa Press ed.
    p.   cm.—(A Bur Oak book)
Originally published: Ames, Iowa: Iowa State
University Press, 1952, 1988.
ISBN-13: 978-1-58729-539-3 (pbk.)
ISBN-10: 1-58729-539-3 (pbk.)
1. Des Moines County (Iowa)—Social life and
customs—19th century.   2. Farm life—Iowa—Des
Moines County—History—19th century.   3. Orchard,
Hugh, 1868–1964—Childhood and youth.   4. Des
Moines County (Iowa)—Biography.   I. Title.
F627.D4O73 2010
977.7'96—dc22   2009048484

Dedicated to my two charming daughters

Annabel Lee and Ruth

who finally convinced me
I should write these recollections

a word to the reader

Memories live on, and here are reminiscences of Iowans and their daily living on a farm in the 1880's as seen through the eyes of a boy. Hugh Orchard has recaptured remarkably the spirit and tempo of this life — reminiscences seasoned with wisdom and salted with humor.

Des Moines County was one of the first settled areas in the state and was no longer a frontier region when the Orchards left Illinois for their new home out in Iowa. Yet in the truest sense, real pioneering remained to be done. Social institutions such as schools and churches had to be given stability and permanence. Costly experiments and heartbreaking adjustments faced this post-frontier generation. In all these, the Orchard family made its contribution. Here is revealed, with unusual clarity, the work of the real builders of modern Iowa — their years of toil; their dreams of better things for their sons.

This is "grass roots history" in the finest sense, for these reminiscences recall the day-to-day adventure of community building. During the years of semi-subsistence agriculture, the farm — even more than in the 1950's — was the center of this experience in rural America. Thus Old Orchard Farm was truly the pivot about which family and community life revolved.

Through the boyish eyes of young Hugh Orchard, the economic hardships of these years do not appear as grim and stark as in our history books. Yet the numerous experiments on Old Orchard Farm to introduce new methods of soil culture, new crop strains, better livestock breeds, and labor-saving machinery reveal the efforts of the Orchards to produce more for less.

It was in this rural community, like thousands of others, that our American nationality was forged.

Hugh Orchard has discovered that local history is both interesting and valuable in understanding ourselves. Much of the charm of these reflections lies in the achievement of recapturing a boy's world in which a broken binder becomes a major crisis, a prairie storm a terrifying experience, and a trip to the county seat town a thrilling adventure filled with a thousand delights.

Many readers will want to know what happened to the boy of this story. Like many Iowans of his generation, Hugh Orchard left the farm to seek success in the city. There followed years of public service as a Christian minister and lecturer in the Chautauqua movement where he earned a wide reputation as a gifted speaker and able organizer. In his eighties at the time of this book, Hugh Orchard, with his energy, humor and kindly philosophy, is a tribute to Old Orchard Farm and to his countless friends throughout Hawkeyeland.

Old Orchard Farm gave richly of its bounty to Iowa. From fertile fields were harvested the foods and fibers for America's fast growing wealth. From her sons and daughters came strength for state and nation.

PAUL F. SHARP

a note from the author

You say you never read a preface. Well, I seldom do myself. But this is *different*. And I have a hunch that you're going to read it.

And, too, the book that follows is *different*. It is not chronological. It bends to no pattern. It has no design. It heralds no message. Open it at any page and you will alight upon something of common interest. And you can quit anywhere without great loss. Pretty comfortable, don't you think?

How did I come to write it? I have always been a public speaker (some even say orator). At every conceivable kind of gathering from great conventions, chautauquas, forums, pulpits, down to household parties, I have always used pretty freely the material found in this book.

Enough people urged me to get it into permanent form that I finally decided to try it: "It's a shame to waste it on mere audiences. Give it to the world at large."

In putting down my experiences on paper, I was

amazed at the wealth of material stored away in what Old Ploudin Huggins called my "photographic memory." I was forced to record it in brief style, or write a dozen books. And that's too many books.

The characters named are real people. All have gone to heaven (I hope), and are in no position to talk back. The only fiction is one name substitution, but I refuse to divulge which it is.

I claim no uniqueness for the story. It could just as well be *your* story. It's a kind of sublimated afterglow of life as it was lived before the totalitarians got to monkeying with it.

I still enjoy the sunshine of those years. I see again the beauty of the shifting cloud effects on lazy summer afternoons. I still get a thrill from those long-ago sunrises, and rest and repose as the sun goes down. The peculiar neighborhood folks, the simple pleasures and pastimes, the wholesome labor, the flight of waterfowl, the sober development of the school, the church, the playground, and the oncoming march of every kind of improvement in ways of doing things — all live in memory as a happy deposit of life as it ought to be lived.

HUGH ORCHARD

notes and acknowledgments

Anyone who has ever tried to write a book knows the trials and tribulations that arise. We all freely acknowledge, with gratitude, any chance assistance that may be rendered by friends and well-wishers.

All the facts, fancies, and historical implications had long been stored in my own memory — very precious and a primary element in my life. Yet in telling them, I felt the need of expert advice and counsel.

Paul F. Sharp, of the History Department at Iowa State College, bravely adopted my manuscript as a problem child, and removed all the cockleburs, jimson, Spanish needles, and dog fennel. Marshall Townsend, of the Iowa State College Press, after a careful diagnosis, skillfully injected dosages of literary penicillin and spiritual sulfa, which preserved all the flavor and flush of the original manuscript. John Huseby captured in his drawings the spirit I had put into my words.

A million thanks to Paul and Marshall and John. You made a reporting farmer of a plain plow-boy who hadn't turned a furrow in sixty years.

H. O.

the recollections

at the beginning

How Pap ever was so lucky as to get hold of Old
Orchard Farm was a puzzler to me. It must have been
one of those providences that just come along when you
are not expecting them, and there you are, first thing
you know, all rigged out fit to kill.

Pap was raised in the backwoods of Illinois. He
was brought up to the cooper's trade, doing a little

farming on the side, on the poorest kind of timber soil close to the village of Cooperstown. Away back yonder, before my time, Paps father left him a forty acre stump patch with a log cabin on it and there he and Mother began to raise a family.

Early one spring a stranger came driving up at sundown and asked could he stop for the night. Of course he could in those days. And after supper it came out, as he and Pap were talking, that this stranger owned a quarter section of rich prairie land out in Iowa, which he had preempted from the Government, and he was all ready to trade it for "most anything that would let him move back to where some folks lived."

He allowed that batching on the wild prairie, five or six miles from the nearest neighbor, was too lonesome a job for him. The upshot was that by daylight next morning Pap and that stranger were on the way to Iowa to see that quarter section.

In two weeks they were back with the trade all made. And, as soon as they could get the papers fixed up and their traps together, Pap, Mother, and the five children (this was before I was born) were off for their new home.

That was the luckiest turn anybody ever saw. It led right into peace and plenty, and the chance of a lifetime to build, and set out, and trim, and cultivate, and generally develop a homestead that not only fed us and clothed us and kept us out of mischief, but somehow formed a kind of reservoir of good will and affection inside us that refuses to fade out.

Old Orchard Farm. It was a jolly good one of two hundred acres in section 29, township 74, range 4 west of the 5th principle meridian, in Washington Township, Des Moines County, Iowa. Burlington, 25 miles away, was our county seat, and seemed to me like one of the greatest cities in the world. It had a population of fifteen or twenty thousand.

Pap started in with a quarter section but when some of us boys got big enough to work steady in the fields, he figured he needed forty acres more to keep us busy. So he bought the forty on the east for $8 an acre, paid for it with one crop of wheat and had eighty five dollars left over.

And on that two hundred acre farm and the neighborhood around it was about as good a place as anybody ever saw to grow up and have a good time on.

prairie
madonna

We called our parents Pap and Mother. Where the word Pap came from I never learned. It must have been a Kentucky word, for that is where they both were born. It sounds rather queer to folks now, but it never sounded strange to us. Names such as *papa, father, mama* or *moms* were the ones that seemed odd to us.

They were an odd looking pair, because Pap was so

tall and Mother was so short. Pap was what they called
a *six-footer,* square shouldered and straight as an Indian,
but Mother was shorter than you would think. I don't
remember whether she was ever measured, but she
could stand under my arm when it was held straight
out sideways, and I am five foot seven and a half. So
I reckon Mother must have been about four foot six
inches tall — or short, whichever it was.

But what Mother lacked in height she made up in
width. She was what was called a chunky woman, but
she was as quick on her feet as a cat. No woman ever
lived that could do more work, or do it faster or better.
And it was a blessed thing that she was so peart and
strong for she was the mother of fourteen children,
and she raised them all too. I happened to be the
twelfth one, and Old Hugh Gardner, who owned five
or six farms, told mother that if she would name me
after him, he would make me a present of a farm when
I grew up. But he up and died long before that time
came and I never got the farm. People generally called
me *Huzer* for short, but when I was about six years old
Pap got to taking rubbing treatments for rheumatism
from a magnetic healer named Doctor Paul Caster and
I renamed myself Huzer Orchard Doctor Paul Caster.
After that some called me *Doc,* and some *Huzer,* and
that was the way of it.

Mother never had any handy things to keep house
with like women do nowadays, and had to do everything by hand. She was married at the age of fourteen,
and through the long stretch of thirty years she either

had a baby on her lap or tugging at her skirts for some kind of motherly attention.

But that is only part of the story. She made all our clothes, carded wool, spun yarn, knitted all our stockings, socks, mittens, scarfs, and pulse warmers, a stitch at a time. She mended our clothes when they needed it, darned our worn out stockings, and kept us looking respectable. She roasted the green coffee in the oven, baked the bread, took care of the milk and cream from a dozen cows, filled the coal oil lamps and polished the chimneys, provided three square meals a day every day in the year, fed thrashing hands, helped pick a hundred geese every spring, got the children off to school on time, taught us manners, inspired us, doctored us when we got sick, saved our lives over and over again, and smiled and sang right through it all as though she liked it better than anything else in the world.

And that is not the whole story either. She not only raised fourteen of her own children, but she furnished a home for seven different orphans at different times. Some of these she just gave a home for a year or two, 'til they found a place to stay regular, but some of them lived at our house until they came of age. She treated them all just exactly like she treated us, the kindest and sweetest anybody ever heard about.

How did she manage to do it all? I'm sure I don't know. She was a wonderful woman and there is no way of explaining her. She was a regular bundle of springs, with a great big heart, and as pretty as a picture.

Without any let-up of duties that piled up every day, with no chance to travel hardly a bit, or any sort of change, she just kept on pouring out a regular flood of blessings on children, friends, and strangers alike. No angel in heaven ever had a pleasanter face, or made less complaint about her lot.

Mother raised the average of my parents pretty high. I never cared much for Pap until I was a man, but I always fairly worshipped Mother and would do anything in the world for her. Anybody would that ever knew her.

She had a way of singing at her work, and as she worked all the time, she was singing a good deal of the time. She had a sweet voice, too. Mostly she sang hymns, because there were not so very many other kinds of songs in those days. Long before we knew the meaning of any of them we liked to hear them, and that was I suppose because we knew what a wonderful heart they came out of. They were not a bit like the church songs they sing now. I don't suppose they are sung any more at all.

One she used to sing went like this:

I would not live always, I ask not to stay,
   Where storm after storm rises swift o'er the way,
The few cloudy mornings that dawn on us here
   Are enough for life's trials, enough for its fears.

Right now as I look at those words I can't see so very much to them. But they were set to a tolerably pretty tune, that is, it was pretty when Mother sang it.

The consecrated cross I'll bear
  'Til death shall set me free;
And then go home a crown to wear,
  For there's a crown for me.

That was another one I liked to hear her sing. For quite a spell I didn't catch all the words just right, and understood her to say "cross-eyed bear." But there wasn't anything funny about that at the time. It was one of Mother's songs, and what mattered about the bear's eyes I'd like to know. It was all right any way she sang it.

She knew two or three dozen church songs, and mostly they were kind of sad. But she was never sad herself, but was always seeing the bright side of things. Everything always brightened right up whenever she came around.

She knew several sentimental kinds of ballads too, and some of them had upwards of twenty verses to them. Those songs told a kind of story, and they were mostly saddish too. There was "The Silk Merchant's Daughter." That was a song and a half! There were lovers, and cruel parents, a lost glove, partings and gettings together again and no end of troubles and sadness. And she could sing "Barbery Allen" so gentle and sad-like that you just couldn't keep from crying, that's all. I reckon she knew a dozen of that kind of songs, and I never got tired of hearing them.

Mother, bless her heart, was our saviour. With all that she had to do, she found time to console us and keep us from open rebellion. As it was, four out of five

boys ran away from home as they came to about eighteen.
I was the only one that stuck it out until I came of age.
But that was not for Pap; it was for Mother. I made
up my mind than I would stand anything before I
would make her cry like she did when the older boys
ran away. And I made good at it too but it was kinda
hard sledding sometimes.

Mother even went so far as to find excuses for
Pap. And anybody that could do that, at times, must
have been a saint. I sometimes wonder if there was ever
another such a woman.

It was always the talk of the neighborhood how
easy she could hold a child on her lap. But practice
makes perfect and she had the practice. She always held
the baby on her lap at the table, fed him while she
ate, poured all the tea and coffee, waited on the other
children, minded the flies, and jumped up a dozen
times during the meal to bring more biscuits, milk,
water or perhaps a new jam she had forgotten to put
on the table. Nobody else could have done all that.

Mother never wasted time resting. When she was
not doing the regular work about the house, she mended
clothes or socks. She knitted while visiting with neighbors who dropped in and knitted again every evening
until bedtime. But somehow it never seemed to be
work to her, for she seemed to take a delight in keeping busy.

How I did like to see her spin yarn! Pap kept a
herd of sheep, and took the wool to Northfield, about
twelve miles away, to have it carded. It came back from

the carding mill in big loose skeins with the wool formed together in rolls about as thick as your finger. Mother would mount a skein of this on a holder back of the spinning wheel, thread the spindle and commence to spin. She turned the big wheel by hand, and a little round belt ran down to the spindle and made it whirl. She would feed the carded wool to that spindle, holding it just the right way, and with just the right pull to turn out finished yarn as smooth and even as you ever saw. That was the beginning of dozens of pairs of stockings, socks, and mittens for children who were not very careful with them either, I am sorry to say.

That old spinning wheel had a lovely hum that didn't sound like anything else in the world. Mother would often tune her voice to it and sing a low and lovely song. It was the prettiest music anyone could imagine.

Pap's first name was Anderson, and Mother's was Caroline. She always called him *Annison,* and he called her *Calline.* They never used such words as *husband,* or *wife,* or *my man,* or *my woman* — or *he* or *she* or *it,* for that matter. To each other they were always just plain *Annison* and *Calline,* and I am as sure as can be that they loved each other dearly — a "monstrous lot," to use one of Pap's expressions. They lived together in full partnership and devotion for seventy-four years, and seemed to love each other better all the time.

a

pap

we

couldn't

manage

Pap was what our school teacher called a Stoic. Six feet tall and strong as a horse, he never seemed hungry or thirsty, but was always a big eater and on a hot day could drink almost a gallon of water. He had no special taste for good food and always ate what was placed before him without a word. He never noticed the difference between a big Sunday dinner and a snack!

I never heard him brag about his family, but he never complained either. He was the cock of the walk and everybody knuckled down to him, even in little things that didn't amount to much. But he hardly ever cuffed any of us and he whipped us only for something serious.

He would work fourteen hours a day without complaining that he was tired. Yet he had a funny notion that he had something seriously wrong with him and might collapse at any time. He had a habit of feeling his own pulse, counting the beats and acting as if he expected his heart to stop then and there. As a result, he was taken in by every patent medicine advertisement he read.

Jayne's Almanack was one of his main standbys, for it was filled with remedies. In it he frequently found lots of symptoms that exactly fitted his case. He bought patent medicines by the barrel and they all helped him. Once he heard of a "Rubbing Doctor" who cured without any medicine, and he drove seventy-five miles for treatments. The doctor helped him, of course, and his rheumatism was better for several days after he got home. He would try almost anything in the shape of medicine if somebody recommended it to him.

But his main standby was National Kidney and Liver Cure put up in quart bottles. It sold for a dollar a bottle, six for five dollars. For two or three years he never took anything else. It had a tin lid, with tinfoil wrapped all around the neck, and the whole thing was covered with some kind of straw wrapping. He had to cut two wires and use a special kind of opener to get into it. It was mighty near as good as cider to take, and, with what we sipped of it on the sly, Pap used up two bottles a week. We used to cart the empty bottles off to the creek when a freshet came along and float them down with the muddy water. We called the ceremony the "National Departure."

Pap would take a sudden notion that butter hurt him and not eat a bite of it for a year. Then he would decide that it was meat and for a considerable spell he wouldn't eat any kind of meat. Next he would settle on sugar, and let the sugar bowl go right by him at the table, just like it was poison. It was first one thing and then another. He always claimed that he didn't miss any of these foods a bit.

He never once suspected coffee hurt him and drank it three times a day, every day in the year. I used to like to watch Pap drink coffee. He always poured it out into his saucer to cool, and then drank it from the edge of the saucer. If it wasn't quite cool enough, he would blow his breath over it until it was. Nearly everybody used to do that, even women.

Then the mustache cup was invented and mother got Pap one for Christmas. Up to that time the men folks drank their coffee through their mustaches, and it was quite a problem. After every drink they had to blow or suck on their mustache to get the worst of it off, and they had to wipe it with a handkerchief before they could go on eating. Napkins hadn't showed up yet, to any extent.

But the mustache cup improved coffee drinking a whole lot. About a third of the cup was covered over to hold the mustache back, and a mouth-shaped opening at the edge let the coffee come through. It was a great success right from the start, and every farmer around there who could afford it soon had one. There was only one drawback to it. Some of the mustache cup users got pretty badly scorched before they got the hang of the thing. Joe Mussack burned a big blister on his upper lip the first time he tried his, and tossed it into the wood box and broke it all to smithereens. But as a general rule they worked fine.

Pap had very little education, as far as schooling goes. The frontier settlement in western Illinois, where his parents settled when they came from Kentucky, didn't have any schools like we have today. Once in a while some person who could read and write would start a private school for a short time in the winter time, but Pap's folks never did take much stock in that. His own daughter, when she was sixteen years old, taught him to read, but he always whispered out loud everything he read and ran his finger along under the words. He had to spell out all but the little words. When he came to a really big word, he just passed it up and went on. The Bible and *Jayne's Almanack* were his basic reading materials and hard as it was for him, he read the Bible through three times from cover to cover, spelling out pretty nearly all of it.

When Pap was reading that was all that was going on about the house, too. And when I say all, I mean all. The least little movement or noise disturbed him bad, and he was liable to lose his line. We soon learned to be quiet as mice when Pap was spelling out his Bible.

It was the same whenever he chanced to lie down on the lounge for a noonday nap. You could have heard a pin drop, not because he ordered it that way, but because he was boss around the place, and all his whims had to be respected to the limit. He had a will of iron and never would stand any kind of contradiction from young or old. He was a regular Andy Jackson, I imagine. Once when somebody told him he was wrong about something, he got red in the face and replied, "I don't pretend to be wrong about nothing."

But he had his good points as well. He was a pioneer in many ways. He bought the first reed organ in our neighborhood and our house soon became a meeting place for youngsters who wanted to sing with that organ. Pap loved to sing and had his own favorites.

He knew some of the funniest songs anybody ever heard. I wish you could have heard him sing "The Beautiful Boy." It was a fool song that had to be acted out to get the flavor — funny faces and curious postures — and Pap could do it just right, little as you might think it. It was big fun for him to sing that song to children, and nervous grownups for that matter, because when they got all wrapped up in the performance, without knowing it they would commence making the same kind of faces and grimaces he did. It was better than a picture show and fifty years ahead of it.

How I would like to find all the words of his favorite songs, "Pompey Smash." It was a wonderful song about a powerful colored hunter named Pompey Smash who told about his adventures and how he came to know everything and everybody.

The world is made of mud and the Massyssippi ribber,
The sun's a ball of foxfire as you may diskibber.

Tell you bout a hunt that I had with Davy Crockett,
Half hoss, half coon and half sky rocket."

Pompey Smash seems to have thought a heap of the great backwoodsman, Crockett, or else he just lauded Crockett so it would seem more important to know him.

Says I, where's your gun? Says he, I ain't none,
Says I, how kin you ketch a coon unless ye got one?

Never do you mind, Sir, but come along with Davy,
Mighty soon show you how to grin a coon crazy.

After trailing the great Davy through the woods jabbering all the time of his hunting exploits,

He stopped right still and begin fer me to feel,
Says he, Pompey Smash, let me brace again yer heel.

I stuck back my heel fer to brace up the sinner,
I see Davy Crockett grin hard fer his dinner.

But the critter kept a eatin' and didn't seem to mind it,
Never stopped a chawin' and never looked behind it.

At last Davy said, It shorely must be dead,
Fer I seed the bark fly all about the critter's head.*

---

* This is a version of the "Ballad of Davy Crockett" which by the mid-nineteenth century had become a favorite Negro minstrel and appeared in almost every theatre in the Midwest.

After more big talk between the two great hunters, they discovered that it was not a coon at all, but just a pine knot on a big stick, and Davy had actually grinned all the bark off of it. It was a wonderful song for a youngster. I don't know how many verses it had, but there must have been forty. We were always sorry when the end came.

Pap was a great story teller too. He didn't know many stories, but the ones he did tell were whoppers. We liked to hear him tell about hunting jayhaws. Not the Jayhawkers of today's stories, but just jayhaws — whatever they were.

Pap had a Kentucky squirrel rifle he named Old Dalsey. When he was telling his jayhawk stories he would go through all the motions of loading the gun with powder, patching and ball and then ram the ball down the barrel. Then he would fish a cap from a pocket and carefully put it on the tube. When he got to the place to shoot he would pretend to lift Old Dalsey up to place her over the limb of a tree. He said jayhawks could be found only on the darkest of nights and then only in the tops of the tallest trees. How we ate up that story when he came walking in with two dozen jayhawks tucked in his vest pocket!

Then he used to tell one about going bat-fowlin'. I can remember every word of that one to this day. His story ran like this:

An old man and old woman went bat-fowlin', one on one side the fence and one on one side. Did you ever hear it?

We would answer *no,* that we had never heard it. Then he would solemnly repeat:

An old man and old woman went bat-fowlin', one on one side the fence and one on one side. Did you ever hear it?

Then all together we would protest that we had never heard it. "Well, well, well," he would say and then maybe get his tobacco pouch out and carefully light his pipe, puff a few times wasting time while we were just bustin to get the end of the story. Then Pap would start all over again:

An old man and old woman went bat fowlin', one on one side the fence and one on one side, are you sure you never heard it?

By this time some of the boys would begin to suspect something and begin to snicker a little. They would look at each other and giggle, finally catching on that all there ever was to the story was that an old man and woman went bat-fowlin' one on one side of the fence and one on *one* side. Then the first time a new bunch of kids came to our house to play he would get them all mixed up and excited with the same story. But in course of time it became known to everybody and just naturally died out, for there weren't enough children in the whole township to keep it going on forever.

Pap was wonderful in amusing little children. He liked them all, bounced them on his knees, sang to them and got a lot of pleasure out of their company. But when his own children got big enough to begin working about the place he seemed to back off, and quit noticing them altogether and became boss.

He was a hard boss who seemed to delight in keeping us busy with hard work. But on a farm there was always work to do and he kept us busy without making any work for us. He never liked his boys to go out sparking girls Sunday nights because it made them sleepy next day and they couldn't get their work done. He always made his own girls send their company home early in the evening for the same reason. We almost hated him for this at times, and I do not like to think of it now. It was so useless for him to act that way.

But Pap was a wonderful man, too, as I found out after I was married and had moved away from home. During the whole period of my years at Old Orchard Farm, however, I never saw him except as a big, stubborn boss. And it was that way with my older brothers as well. Joe and Frank always called him "Bonco," but they never let him hear them. I never learned what that word meant, but I sensed it was very uncomplimentary.

One time when I was visiting the boys as they were plowing corn, Joe sent Frank to the house for a fresh jug of water. When he returned Joe asked, "Where is Bonco?"

"Settin' there in the shade, suckin' his old pipe and tryin' to read," was the unsympathetic answer. But it was Pap's fault, for he never could understand youngsters and we never could understand him.

He started to whip me once when I was sixteen

years old. I was about full grown and he ought to have known better than try to humiliate me in that fashion. Up to this time I had been docile, obeying his orders and respecting his wishes, but now I was beginning to feel my oats. We were out in the field together replanting corn with hoes. I was using an old grubbing hoe that weighed six or seven pounds while Pap had a light one, the handle of which had been half burned off in the middle. He had told me repeatedly to hit the ground harder in making a hole to plant the corn, but the heavy grubbing hoe sank deep enough into the ground of its own weight. So I would hit the ground fairly hard when he was looking and do as I pleased when he was not.

Finally he caught me at my deception and yelled out from a distance of fifty yards, "Hugh, I shan't speak to you again." Then raising his light hoe high in the air he brought it down with great force, shouting at the same time, "Bring your hoe down like this."

But Pap had put entirely too much enthusiasm into his demonstration and the hoe handle broke at the burned place. Before I knew what I was doing I tauntingly shouted, "Yes, indeed," and then burst out laughing.

That was too much for Pap. With a roar he came running, waving the fragment of the hoe handle and sputtering, "Ain't that a nice way for a boy to treat his father?"

"And that's a nice way for a father to treat a son," I shouted right back.

He was mad as a hornet and so was I to think that he would try to whip me when I was this big. So I stood there planning what to do, but there was little time for thought and I probably did the wrong thing. In any case, I raised the grubbing hoe as if to use it in defense and stood my ground. My plan was to stand him off with a bluff, if it worked, and if it didn't I planned to run with all my might — for I knew I could outrun him and get away.

But he stopped about ten feet from me, turned on his heel and walked back to his broken hoe which he picked up and took to the house. When I went in for dinner he was in bed with a high fever and lay there several days. When finally he got over it and began to mix with us again I expected him to do something to square the account. He never did, however, and that was the last time he ever tried his hand on me. The next time we locked horns cured him completely. It was this way.

I had a girl living in Sperry, fifteen miles away. It was a long ride on horseback, and it was hard to plan satisfactory hours with her and yet tend to the farm chores at the regular time. Like most boys, I was inclined to let the chores slide on Sunday evenings and let the pigs get fed as best they could or wait until the following morning. It would never hurt them, I always told myself.

On this particular occasion I had borrowed John Cappes' buggy and was hitching a span of three year old colts as I dreamed of the grand time I was soon to enjoy. My pleasant revery was interrupted by the unpleasant sound of my father's voice asking me where I thought I was going. I told him I was going to Sperry. "To see that whiffet of a girl, I suppose," he exploded. But I kept my temper and refused to answer him, for Mother was within hearing distance and I didn't want to say something that would hurt her.

I hitched the last trace and started to climb into the buggy when Pap came charging out toward me with the command to unhitch the horses and turn them into the pasture. "Get a girl close home," he shouted, "so you can be here to do the chores on time."

This made me mad clean through, and when a fellow gets to that pitch he isn't afraid of anything and doesn't care very much for the consequences. Quick as a flash I landed in the buggy and gave the word to the horses. Pap came running and took them by the bits, determined to frustrate my plans. But I poured the whip into the colts and they reared right up on their hind legs as if they were going to jump over him. This forced him to duck out of the way. As I turned to drive off he yelled after me, "You be back at sundown to do the chores or you can settle with me." All I did was shake my head.

The farther I drove the madder I got and the more precious my Doxie Jane seemed to me. This lasted ten miles or more, but by the time I got to Sperry I had cooled off considerable. But I couldn't think of anything else all afternoon and my girl noticed something was wrong, but I never told her what.

When the time came to start for home I put my team in a livery stable and went to bed. I stayed at my girl's house until ten o'clock the next day, then I started leisurely homeward, for I wanted to be late. I craved an encounter with Pap that would put an end to this sort of thing. I drove into the barnyard full of fight and honing for trouble. I unharnessed the colts, turned them loose in the pasture and went into the house to change into my working clothes. But Pap had gone to Yarmouth without even mentioning our tilt. Mother, however, feared that trouble was brewing. And I hoped she was right.

When I came in from the field that evening Pap was in the barn lot waiting and asked me something or other about the corn. To my complete surprise, he chatted pleasantly about his trip into town. Two things bothered me. I had supposed that he would be in bed with another fever, and I had imagined he would settle with me as he had threatened. Neither one happened.

After that we got along fine as a fiddle, though we didn't do much talking. I began to take a liking to Pap as soon as I had him licked and he quit trying to bully me. After I was married and got to going back home to visit I fell in love with him, for I discovered he was a most entertaining host, a gentle and kind-hearted man. He just never had learned to get along with children. It cost him dearly, as it cost us all.

And I don't want to say that Pap was always ornery

to us. He had his good streaks as well as anybody. He was a wonderful provider for his family, he taught us the value of work, and was as honest as the day was long.

Pap had always asked the blessing at the dinner table with exactly the same words.

"Oh, Lord, bless us, save us all in Heaven. We ask for Christ the great Redeemer's sake, Amen."

Three times daily for sixty years Pap said that blessing. We all had it memorized, of course, but we bowed our heads and were as quiet as mice while he said it.

Sundays or when we had guests, he had a somewhat different blessing: *"Oh, Lord, bless us all as thou seest we need. Go with us through the journey of life, pardon and forgive us all our sins and at last in Heaven save us. We ask for Christ the great Redeemer's sake, Amen."* That was all the praying I ever heard Pap do. I guess he and Mother both tried to live up to what Christ taught about doing your praying in secret. And I still think that is about the right way. A heap of the praying one hears sounds just like it was fixed up for people to hear instead of God, and I reckon that kind never gets much higher than people's heads.

We got a lot of fun out of Pap's queer ways. Once he bought a jackass, and was all fired up over the business of raising a flock of mules. He wasn't satisfied to treat that animal like other folks but insisted on driving him hitched to the road cart. It was a funny sight with Pap perched up behind that diminutive, long-eared ass riding along at a snail's pace on the roadway.

The village of Yarmouth was but two miles away and it took Pap over an hour to drive that donkey there. He could make the trip back in thirty or forty minutes, for it was down hill most of the way and the donkey wanted to get back to his hay. Once Pap hitched this animal to a single shovel cultivator and tried to plow the potato patch with him. He didn't have any luck keeping the animal in the row and the donkey walked over so many hills that Pap either had to give up or call for help. Since Pap never gave up, he called my sister Belle to come out and lead the beast while he held the plow handles.

But that jackass didn't lead any better than he drove. He would lower his big, burly head and go heaving recklessly along, trampling the finest row of potatoes in the patch. At the end of the row he would head right into the garden fence and twice he fairly butted Belle over. He was so unruly, dumb and awkward that she had a hard time keeping him from stepping on her feet. Finally Belle started to cry, so Pap got one of the big boys to take her place. Frank jumped on the jack's back, wrapped his long legs around him, cuffed him over the ears and put him through the patch at such a speed that Pap had to run to keep up. Altogether they trampled a third of the plants and plowed under another third. But it was a good year and we had all the potatoes we needed despite that donkey.

The jackass never satisfied Pap. On the advice of

a neighbor named Lander, he put the animal in a dark stall and fed him a diet of potato peelings. It always seemed to me that Lander meant a stall that was slightly darkened and a diet of potato peelings mixed with grain, but Pap took the advice literally and chinked up all the cracks in an old log crib, making it as dark as the inside of a cow. It took all our men to force the jack into that dark hole, but we finally overcame him and latched him in. For months Pap had all the neighbor women saving potato peelings for him and the only daylight that poor donkey saw was when Pap opened the door to give him a pail of water and his peck of potato peelings.

But instead of doing better the jack did worse and got as scrawny as a sick rabbit. When Pap finally decided to let him out, the donkey was as blind as a bat, his eyes stayed sore for weeks and his ears sunburned badly. Pap then fixed a half-darkened stall and put the donkey on a Christian diet that had him back on his feet in a short time. But Pap never admitted his error and soon got rid of the donkey, thus removing the visible evidence of his folly. Pap never did things by halves.

He had a keen sense of humor, too, but kept it pretty well in the background while we were children. He used to tell about a man he hired once to cut a field of wheat with a cradle. The man kept complaining that the cradle did not hang to suit him. So Pap took a wrench and shifted the blade for him, but the man still complained that it failed to suit him. Pap changed the position of the handles, but the man still complained that it did not suit his tastes. In desperation Pap took the cradle to the blacksmith and had it adjusted all over so that it was just like a new one. But the fellow still complained that it did not hang to suit him. Finally, in disgust, Pap told the man to hang it for himself and see if he could do it any better. The man walked over to a tree and hung the cradle on a limb. There it hung to suit him exactly.

Pap also liked to tell of the time he engaged another man to cut wheat. The man came at sunrise and began immediately to whet the blade of the cradle. He whetted until called for breakfast, after eating he commenced to whet some more. He whetted, and whetted and whetted. About ten o'clock Pap went out to see how the man was getting on with the work, but there the fellow stood under the shade of a tree still whetting. Pap scolded him for not getting to work in the field but the man replied, "there is nothing lost by whettin'."

He whetted until dinnertime without cutting a straw of wheat. Pap told him he was a fool and that he would never pay for time wasted in such fashion. But the man only turned his warnings aside with the reply, "there is nothing lost by whettin'." After dinner he went out and began to whet some more. Pap checked again at three o'clock only to discover that the man was still whetting. Pap tried to dismiss the foolish worker, but he just grinned and reassured him that "there is nothing lost by whettin'." When Pap returned to supper and the man hadn't cut a single swath but protested loudly that "there is nothing lost by whettin'," Pap was so disgusted he refused to talk to the man at all.

But after supper the man took up his cradle and began to fell the golden grain with long sweeps. Around and around the field he flew, laying the cradlefuls in straight swaths ready for the rakers and binders. Just as the sun went down Pap went out to see what was going on. He discovered that the man had completed the ten acre field and, having finished at the far end, was headed toward the house cutting six rows of corn as he came. When he came in he winked his eye at Pap and muttered with a chuckle, "there is nothing lost by whettin'."

Some of Pap's stories sounded familiar, but we enjoyed them anyway. Like most of us he sometimes slipped in the personal pronoun when it was not required, and he was never guilty of ruining a good story by strictly sticking to the facts.

grandpa emerick and his son-in-law

Grandpa Emerick lived about forty rods up the road from our house and I guess he was one of the most wonderful men that ever lived. He was my mother's father and was an old man when I first knew him. But he must have had young ideas, for he was a regular picnic for us kids.

His name was John Emerick, and he was of German extraction, although he didn't speak German much. He was a six footer, and nobody ever knew how strong he was. In pioneer days, in Brown county, Illinois, he was one of the men relied on by the community to fight for the peace and order of the settlement. And a lot of fist fighting had to be done then. There was no law of any account, and bullies had to be taken down whenever they got to be too troublesome.

He used to love to relate his early exploits, especially at election times when whiskey flowed like water and as many as a dozen fights — or more — occurred during the day's voting. The people mostly had mighty little notion of what the election was all about, but they were ready to fight for their candidates at the drop of a hat. Grandpa used to tell how, in one of these fights, he disposed of seven men in turn, and the eighth was badly beaten by my Pap. Pap was then a young man and had his adversary down, pounding him on the bottom of the foot when Grandpa broke up the fight. Pap had pounded his victim all over and was just finishing up on the unusual spot. Grandpa never tired of telling that story.

During another particularly exciting election Grandpa was campaigning for Justice of the Peace as usual. Midway in the campaign Sam Griggs came to him with the news that Pete Schomp was spreading lies about him and that he had better do something about it. Grandpa's answer was a hearty laugh. He told Griggs that as long as Schomp confined himself to spreading lies he wouldn't get excited. But if Schomp ever got to telling the truth, it certainly would lose him the election. That was his way of laughing off the troubles that others worried about.

He was not a great farmer, but put in a good deal of his time selling patent rights, books, and trinkets. He drove a team of ponies and a rickety old buggy which you could hear coming for half a mile. He always called his ponies *tackies*. He hitched up the tackies. He drove the tackies. He swapped tackies. I never heard anybody else call them that, it was just his word, I guess.

Grandpa never had much formal schooling, but he had a good education. He served as Justice of the Peace for forty years, writing out all the deeds and other legal papers by hand, since in those days there were no blanks or forms provided by the government. He kept all his court records, docket and legal forms in pen and ink. He married hundreds of people, sent a good many to jail, assessed fines and settled a whale of a lot of disputes out of court. All in all, he was one of the valuable and important citizens of our little community.

He loved to tell us of his school experiences, limited as they were. In his day the only text books were a blue-backed speller and a New Testament. The speller was a composite kind of book combining reading and spelling with some arithmetic thrown in for good measure. Grandpa always claimed that his schooling was confined to three days: "The first day I forgot to take my book. The second day the teacher wasn't there. On the third day I didn't go myself."

He and Grandma lived with us while he was getting ready to go out to Nebraska to take up a homestead. It was better than a winter's schooling to hear him tell his stories. He had a wonderful fund of information and the imagination to supply whatever else was needed to make him one of the most interesting men you ever saw.

Born on the Virginia border, he was taken by his parents at an early age to the wilds of Kentucky where he grew to manhood. When that country got crowded he moved to Brown County, Illinois. There he helped to clear away the forest, build log cabins, fight Indians, operate a cooperage and lay the foundations of a civilized community. Here he married and here his children were born, but he tired of this place too and moved on to Iowa. Since the Hawkeye state was then very young, he went through the same kind of pioneering again. Strangest of all, at the age of eighty he moved again! This time he went to Nebraska, filed a claim on a tract of government land, lived on it in bachelor's quarters for three long years and proved his claim at the age of eighty-three. We always claimed him as one of the oldest homesteaders in American history.

Grandma had died in the meantime and was buried at Pleasant Grove cemetery where there was an old country church of their denominational persuasion. Grandpa came back to see us at the end of his Nebraska experience. He got off the train at New London, about ten miles from Old Orchard Farm, and hunted up one of our neighbors in town. It was the dead of winter so the two started for home in a great bobsled, all wrapped up in horse blankets against the bitter cold. Charlie Kemery, the neighbor, later said that Grandpa was in high spirits, relating many a fine story of pioneer days and his part in them. As they rode along Grandpa raised his hand and proudly pointed to a piece of land that he once had owned. Suddenly and without warning he exclaimed, "I am dying." Kemery stopped the horses and tried to hold Grandpa in the seat, but he was too heavy and crumpled into the bottom of the wagon box. Kemery stopped at the next house but Grandpa was dead. He had come home to die and be buried with his beloved Beckie in the Pleasant Grove lot.

It was a shock to all of us. I remember that I came home fifteen miles from the little country school where I was teaching, to attend the funeral. Although the roads were blocked with snow and slush there was a great crowd of neighbors to pay their tribute to one of the last of the true pioneers. The procession was almost a mile long. The preacher conducting the funeral didn't come anywhere near capturing the meaning of Grandpa's restless life. But of course the preacher had never known Grandpa Emerick and didn't know all the good things he could tell.

Folks used to say that I resembled Grandpa Emerick. It always tickled me to hear them say that, for there never was a man I would rather take after than him.

friends
and
neighbors

Though I didn't pay much attention to it at the time, I know now that there were a good many odd people in our neighborhood, with a lot of curious ways.

Old Joe Mussack was the iron man of our community, a great big fellow, strong as an ox and a horse for work. He took such pride in his strength that sometimes it was a little hard for the other men to take. At thrashing time he always insisted on working out in the shock field and would actually pitch a whole shock of grain onto a wagon in one forkful. Other men pitched one bundle at a time, and that gave the loader a chance. But not Joe. He would nearly bury the loader alive, so the other men tried every way they could to avoid his station.

Joe's front teeth were double and he liked to startle folks — especially strangers — by chewing chicken bones and tough foods which other people would leave on their plates. He could neither read nor write except to sign his name. His oldest boy taught him how to scrawl *Joe Mussack* so it could be made out, and that was the extent of his formal schooling.

Both he and his wife were over six feet tall and all their children grew to be that tall too.

He had to have fork handles and ax handles made extra strong and they say he could hold up a ten gallon keg of beer and drink out of the bunghole. Once he carried home on his shoulder all the way from Yarmouth — a distance of four miles — a wooden pump with twenty feet of spouting on it. It must have weighed 150 pounds and he never set it down once. He never had any fights, for there wasn't any use for anybody to try to lick a man like that. "Strong as Old Joe Mussack" came to be a common saying.

On the next farm south of Mussacks lived Old Tom Darbyshire and his family. He was a rough, loud-mouthed Englishman nobody could ever quite figure out. Though celebrated for his cussing, his profanity was confined mostly to just two words: "By Goll!" But he said it so often, no matter what the subject was, that he got the reputation of being one of the cussingest men in the world.

He always had a fuss on with his livestock. Early in the mornings or late in the evenings we could hear Old Tom, whooping and yelling at his cattle and hogs and "By Golling" them something fierce. He always seemed uncomfortable and fretting at something like a hayseed down his back or sand in his boots.

His wife, Aunt Emily as everybody called her, was as quiet and as sweet and as nice as anyone could be. She was very religious, and to her every piece of poetry was a prayer. She used to clip every little verse she saw in the newspaper and paste it in a book. She took a lot of pleasure in showing these poems to people who dropped in.

"That's a pretty little prayer" she would say, handing over a verse, though like as not it was a thousand miles from a prayer. But no matter what the subject was, if it was in rhyme it was a pretty little prayer to Aunt Emily.

Old Tom taught us one thing we never forgot. It was not much in itself, but it stuck like a cocklebur in our memories. It was one of his odd habits at the family table. If there was something that Tom wanted which happened to be out of his reach he never bothered to ask for it. He would simply stand up in his place at the table, reach across the table and spear it with his fork. If it happened to be fat meat, it might drip all the way across to his plate. But it did not seem so bad in those days, for most women used oil-cloth instead of table cloths.

Tom would do the same thing at anybody's house when he would be there helping to thrash or raise a barn. We thought it was funny and we children used to mock him when the old folks were away and nobody was looking. "Tommin' " we called it. And I never to this day see anybody make a long reach at the table without thinking of Old "By Goll" Tom Darbyshire.

Then there was John Conklin, bellwether of the Baptist church. John always raised all the money to pay the preacher and served as Sunday School super-intendent for forty years. He always talked very proper, and always ate with napkins, glass goblets and pearl-handled knives and forks on the table. When his boys grew older they persuaded him to change the spelling to Conkling because they thought it looked more im-pressive that way.

One thing gave John a strange appearance, and came from his habit of always wiping his mustache the same way, from left to right. In time it got to grow-ing that way. Generally a mustache parts in the middle and sprangles off evenly both ways. But John's mus-tache all headed toward his right ear. We got used to it of course, and John would have looked queer to us any other way. They were fine folks, of course, but there was a general feeling that maybe they thought themselves a little above common folks.

John Tucker was our neighborhood mystery man.

Mystery surrounded his whole family, for nobody was ever able to get acquainted with any of them. The Tuckers never mixed with the rest of us to any great extent. Neighborhood gossips whispered that Tucker was a bootlegger and the Funk boys, his immediate neighbors on the west, always claimed he acted like a detective. A good many people were afraid that some day Tucker would break loose and harm someone.

Once our folks saw him digging a hole in his field along a line fence. This started the rumor that he might have murdered someone and was disposing of the body. Late that night several neighbors gathered, went to the spot and dug into the fresh dirt, but they couldn't find a trace of anything suspicious. That only deepened the mystery!

Pete Funk was another mysterious figure. As far back as I can remember he had been kept locked up in his bedroom, because of insanity. All of us youngsters were afraid Pete might get loose and catch us. Whenever we saw a man walking alone through the fields we ran for home, fearing that it was Funk.

Pete had three boys, Pete, Henry and Lou. They were good, honest and hard working German boys, but they had an odd manner of using their breath as they talked. Ordinarily people talk with just the breath that is going out, but the Funk boys used it both ways — perhaps to save it, maybe.

Henry once told of a hunting exploit when he fired a shot that killed a brant and two or three ducks. "The other boys shot and shot," he said, "but they didn't

kill anything. I shot and killed a brant and two ducks."
Up to the word *brant* he spoke normally, using the out-
going breath, but he finished the sentence from there
on while inhaling. Try that yourself and see how
funny it sounds. One of our steady sources of amuse-
ment was to engage the Funk boys in conversation to
watch them do double duty with their breath.

We had two men in our school district by the name
of Oberman. Both were John Oberman and heads of
families. True to country form we invented means of
telling them apart. One we called "High John" Oberman because he claimed to be high German and the
other we called "Dried-Up Johnny" Oberman because
he was so little and skinny. High John was an educated
German who had escaped from the Fatherland in dis-
guise and we confidently waited for the time when he
would be hauled back for service in the German army.
His sober countenance and his fine manners put him
pretty high. He could have been elected to any office
up to Justice of the Peace, I imagine. But he never
seemed to have any hankering for public office.

Dried-Up Johnny raised his family on a rough and
hilly farm at the edge of the tall timber. They were
pretty poor and their children sometimes came to
school with pretty slim lunches. But Dried-Up Johnny
had a way of curing meat that made it taste wonderful.
I can recall to this day the smell of that dried meat the
kids sometimes brought to school. Then sometimes we
would trade our common fodder for a bite of that dried
meat. Oh, but it was good! We could taste it for hours

and we learned not to take a drink of water for the rest of the day, just so we could keep that good taste.

Over behind our fields in a clapboard shanty lived an interesting family by the name of Perkins. We never heard the old man's Christian name, he was just called Perkins. He had a fat, soft and shabby appearing wife and several scarecrow-like children. They were a shiftless lot with too great a fondness for hunting and fishing ever to amount to much. They always had three or four dogs, a couple of old guns, an old grey mare, a one-horse democrat and several stands of bees — that was about all. The old man used to hire out for wages at harvest and corn picking time for a few dollars to live on. Just how they managed to get along nobody knew.

Old man Perkins had a habit of disappearing for sometimes as long as ten days or two weeks, but his family seemed to get used to it and never worried about it. His children never seemed to care very much for him, maybe because he was always bearded, ragged, lazy and shiftless.

Once he tried to find out from his son Jeff how he stood in comparison with a dog they owned.

"Jeff," he asked, "If I should take Watch and go away off, and be gone for a considerable spell, which would you be lonesomest for, me or Watch?"

"I'd druther see Watch," said Jeff.

One winter night there was a loud knocking at our front door. Pap, who was always a light sleeper, jumped out of bed to see who was there at that time of night.

We heard him say, "Why hello, Jeff, what in blazes you doin' here this time of night?" Jeff replied that he had come to borrow a saw.

"Borrow a saw!" said Pap in great surprise. "What in the world do you need of a saw in the middle of the night?" Jeff stammered that they wanted it to cut the hatchway bigger, that the old man was caught tight in it and they couldn't get him down.

By this time we boys had our duds on and were ready for an adventure. Pap got the saw and we hurried across the field to the Perkins shanty. A dim tallow candle shone through the front window as we approached.

"What's up?" Pap asked of Mrs. Perkins when she opened the rickety door.

"We found Pa dead in the loft," the old lady replied, "and we been tryin' to get him down. He's been gone ten days I reckon, but we didn't think nothing of that, he bein' gone that way a lot. But yisteday I snifted something not jest right in the house, and tonight it got so bad I sent Jeff up into the loft to see what he could find out. And there lay Pa as dead as a mackerel."

"Well, well, well," Pap said, and then the old lady went on: "So the boys commenced right away to git him down, and did git him part way through the hatch-hole, but he was puffed up some, you see, and one arm kinder ketched back someway, and he stuck tight right where he is now."

It was a mess. Pap climbed up on a stool and sawed several boards off, and we all got hold and hefted the old man to the floor. There was no such thing as an undertaker in those days, so Pap laid out the corpse on some boards laid across a couple of chairs. Then he offered to take the old lady and the children home with him for the night. It was arranged that two of us boys were to stay at the Perkins' cabin to watch the corpse. So the old lady washed out a pair of woolen socks and hung them before the fireplace to dry and asked us to slip them on Pa when they got dry.

It was kinda creepy sitting away over there back of the fields, off the main road, in the flicker of a tallow candle in the middle of the night and with a dead man for company. But we never blinked and sleep was the farthest from our minds. We kept pretty still somehow — stiller than you would think boys could be. After quite a spell of that we got an idea. Frank suggested that we might as well put the old man's socks on now. Being dead he wouldn't catch cold and what was the difference. I agreed that I could see no difference so we got the wet socks and commenced to put them on.

Now anybody who has tried to put wet socks on knows that they go on hard. We pulled and tugged and finally upset the contraption he was laid on and his body plumped right down on the floor. After that it was less trouble to get the socks on him, and we lifted him back into position on the pine boards and put the sheet over his face again. By that time it was beginning to get daylight, so we got our things on and headed for home. We were glad to leave, too.

The Perkins family couldn't afford a burial lot in

the graveyard, so we buried the old man on a little knoll
not far from the shanty he died in. Mrs. Perkins said
she had never before been so satisfied about Pa. Now
she knew where he was, day or night.

The Perkinses were not altogether useless. The old
man had been extra help at harvest time and corn picking, he sometimes drove around peddling fish, and often
he would cut a bee tree in the woods and peddle the
honey. They were clever about borrowing things, and
when the smallpox epidemic came along they furnished
three cases. We boys used to put Jeff through experiments that we thought were a little too risky for us. We
learned from Jeff about the harmlessness of green apples
as a diet. Mother had always warned us against eating
them and taught us that "one green apple will put your
teeth on edge; two will give you cholera morbus; three
will kill you dead." We heard that so often that we could
say it forward and backward and sideways. With great
courage we would eat two and a half apples, then grave-
ly ponder the question of what could be in that other
half apple that could be so deadly.

One day we coaxed Jeff into eating three green
apples. He not only obliged us by eating three, but went
right on and ate three more for good measure. Then he
jumped onto his old horse and rode off with no in-
tention of falling dead from cholera morbus or anything
else. We watched him ride away, expecting to see him
tumble from his horse, but instead he came riding back
in a short while with a rag and some salt in it. To our
horror he chomped down several more green apples on

top of the six he had already eaten. And they were even better with salt!

That exploded the warning about the deadly effects of green apples. From then on we ate all we could swallow and, except for an occasional stomach ache, suffered no bad effects. But Mother was right. At least she thought she was and nobody could ever make me believe that she would try to deceive us, even for our own good.

Perkinses had a married daughter who lived with her worthless husband down on the river bottom. They never got much of a start in life, except with babies, and they had five of them by the time they had been married seven years. Lots of folks helped them every winter and mother always sent clothes after we had outgrown them. Occasionally she sent Nora one of her own dresses to make over.

Once when her good for nothing husband was peddling fish through the neighborhood, Nora came along to visit us. She was wearing one of the dresses Mother had given her. It was the funniest fitting dress we had ever seen, for it hung almost six inches longer in the front and puffed out at the shoulders so that Nora looked like a hunchback. We just couldn't keep from laughing at her.

Mother spoke up and said. "Nora, what in the world have you done to the dress? I thought you were about the same size as my girl Edith and that it would fit you good."

"Well," drawled Nora, "it buttons up the back and

I couldn't nurse the baby without turning it around. So I put it on hind part before."

Mother made her take off the dress and in five minutes had it all fixed so that Nora could wear it correctly with a slit in front for nursing the baby. But Nora had been too ignorant or shiftless to figure out how to do that for herself.

Another neighbor we thought rather odd was named Peckham. Nobody pretended to know very much about him. He was a tall, pale, rawboned and lonesome man. He owned the wettest, levelest and soggiest farm in the county. Some claimed that Peckham had web feet like a duck, but we never took much stock in that. He would work all day with a crowd of neighbors on some community project without saying a word. Our school teacher said that Peckham was silent as a Sphinx and I think everybody was a little afraid of him.

Altogether there were enough odd people in our neighborhood to furnish us all the diversion we needed, but perhaps we may have seemed strange at times to them also.

pierkses two boys, one of 'em

"I'm Pierkses two boys, one of 'em."

That was the answer he gave to Pap's question as he bounced along on horseback close behind our democrat on the way home from Yarmouth one Saturday night.

It was this way. Henry Pierks, who lived in a cabin at the edge of the woods a few miles farther on, had two boys about fourteen and sixteen years old. From the time they were little fellows they were always together, went places together, worked together and wherever one was, there the other was too. It got to be funny. Our Sunday School teacher always said that "the Pierkses boys are inseparable." And that was about it.

I do not remember that I ever heard either of their given names. They were just "Pierkses two boys," and somehow we got to thinking of them as twins.

On this Saturday night the brothers had got separated in the crowd and one of them was galloping home alone. As was the custom in those days of friendly informality, Pap turned and called, "Hello, there, who might you be?"

Quick as a flash the answer came back, "I'm Pierkses two boys, one of 'em."

Pap laughed right out loud and we kids giggled. The more we thought about it the funnier it seemed. And it has stuck with me through the years as one of the homely incidents that helped to brighten things in a country neighborhood given pretty generally to corn and swine, with a little apple cider on the side.

Through the years I have completely lost sight of the Pierkses, along with many of the others. If the two boys are still living I hope they have managed to stay together. If dead, I hope they lie side by side. They live, in memory, along with Old Joe Mussack, Dan Michaels, Tom Darbyshire, Pete Funk, Chauncey Blodgett, Conrad Bombey, John Tucker, Pete Schomp, Sam Griggs, John Emerich, Pete Cappes and Peckham as fine neighbors and good friends.

This short list of folks has a striking number of Petes in it. Not one of them was ever called Peter, for it was country style to shorten every name. Again these names appear strange on the printed page but to us they never seemed odd, for they were typical American names.

This matter of a name led to tragedy in our community. Itsie Wurmser, who attended our district school, was good looking and smart. But she was always sensitive about that name. She felt that *Itsie* was bad enough, but *Wurmser!* Of course, she could always hope to get rid of it some day by getting married but in the meantime it worried her constantly.

Nobody graduated from our school in those days. Students either dropped out to go to work on the farm or in the kitchen, or sometimes simply got too old to go to school any longer. Eventually the time came when Itsie stopped attending school, for she had a "feller" whose name was Adolphus Schlaub — from away up in the country.

The courtship of Itsie and Adolphus progressed handsomely as far as anybody could see and in due time he popped the question. Itsie said yes. Whatever else may have been in her mind, here was a chance to escape the stigma of that name. The future held great promise for her until one Valentine's day she wrote a perfumed note to send to her beloved as a Valentine. Just in fun, and as countless lovers have done, she signed her name Itsie Schlaub. There her world came to an end. Itsie Schlaub! What a mixture of skin irritation and sauerkraut that name proved to be when written on paper!

They found the poor girl dead in her bed the next morning. There was an empty laudanum bottle on the lampstand and a final message of despair. "Itsie Schlaub is even worse than Itsie Wurmser. Goodbye forever."

In a frontier settlement like ours, in the 1880's, the death of any person was an important event. Our best attended gatherings were the funerals. But a suicide! The taking of one's life! It would never do to let such a person be buried without benefit of the presence of the entire community.

A mile-long procession slowly followed the earthly remains of the poor, disappointed Itsie to her grave. Without regard for the cold or the snow-blocked roads they poured in from every part of the community in sleighs, bobsleds, wagons, democrats and road carts of every description. Another hundred or more came on horseback. Not a fourth of the crowd could find room in the little country church and most were forced to stand in the cold outside to speculate on the possible fate of the one who had committed the crime which the preacher said, "left no place for repentance."

In the crowd waiting outside that day were a couple of old cronies named Sam Griggs and Pete Cappes. Since Cappes was deaf as a post, Griggs had to repeat everything to make him understand. As the crowd shivered and milled about we heard Griggs say, "Pete, you can't blame her. I say you can't blame her."

"You say they couldn't tame her?" whispered the deaf Cappes.

"No," replied the exasperated Griggs, "I say you couldn't blame her."

Pete seemed to show some signs of understanding and after a moment of contemplation responded, "No, you didn't name her. Nobody can blame *you*."

Old Pete Cappes — what pleasant memories are revived by the mention of that name. Pete was German through and through. He had run away from the Fatherland to escape military service, bringing his thrifty frau with him and settling on the farm just north of ours.

Mrs. Cappes was one of the most neighborly and kindest women we knew. Was there ever in the world such coffee cake as she could bake! How she enjoyed passing a big slice of it to me over the hedge fence that bordered our field in front of their house when, tired and hungry from the hard work of weeding corn, I would rest in the shade of that hedge. She always insisted that its flavor was better with coffee but I never could understand how it could have been improved on one bit.

Pete Cappes was better than a daily newspaper, and in some ways that was exactly what he was. Since there were no daily papers in those days, Pete reported all the news for us. He knew everything that was going on in the neighborhood, in spite of his deafness, and he liked to tell it to everyone he came across.

In all his years in Iowa he never dropped the German forms of speech. When his hogs killed a number of geese in the barnlot he told us the next day

"The geese eat the hogs up." Or on other occasions he would say, "The cow jumped the fence over" and always he would command, "The stove put some wood in, John." When people began to lay tiling to drain wet land Pete called it "pifin." I guess he tried to say *piping,* but I never knew for sure.

His three boys — Bill, John and Lou — could drive straighter corn rows than anybody else in the neighborhood. Straight corn rows were a matter of great pride and people would drive out of their way to see the corn rows in the Cappes fields. They were perfect. From one end to the other there wasn't a kink in them.

On rainy days the Cappes boys would come strolling across the fields to our house to loaf and visit in the barn. On these days we always mended the harness, sorted corn or fanned timothy seed and they were welcome help. If Pap had gone to town we would pitch horseshoes on the barn floor, using spike nails for pegs. Lots of money was made and lost on those games, but none ever changed hands. Money was scarce in those days.

We had a two year old bull which we kept in the barn but he had to be led out to water twice a day. To keep the bull at a respectable distance we snapped a pole into the nose ring, for he was ugly at times. One day when the Cappes boys came to visit, Frank decided to show off a bit and started to lead the bull to water. Not to be outdone in bravery, John Cappes jumped on the bull's back for a ride.

The bull was mad as a hornet. He made a wild rush

for the door, forgot all about the ring in his nose, and jerked loose from Frank's grip. He busted through the barn door and across the manure pile, all the time doing his best to buck John off. But John slid forward on the bull's neck and grabbed the critter's horns, to hold on. Around and around the barn the bull ran — plunging, bucking and snorting. We could tell that John was scared and wanted off but was afraid to slide down for fear the bull might turn on him. After some of the liveliest sport you ever saw the bull gave up and ran back to his stall. John jumped off pale as a ghost and with his hair on end, but he had really given us a show.

That goes to show how hungry we sometimes got for excitement and how reckless a young fellow can be.

progressive farming

Pap was what today we would call a progressive farmer. He bought the first windmill in our neighborhood and invested in the first blooded bull. He had the first twine binder and the first top buggy. He put up the first barbed wire fence and tried out the first woven wire picket fence. He was the first to use tiling for draining a wet place in the fields and once went a hundred miles to buy a road cart which was the first one any of our neighbors had ever seen.

He was the first to plant Osage hedge for fencing and the first to dig it out when it didn't work. He had the first hay carrier and our old Brown corn planter was one of the early ones. He bought the first sulky rake and the first sulky plow. Some neighbors made slighting remarks about any man who had to ride while he plowed, but Pap only laughed and let them keep on walking.

He was the handiest man about doing things. His ax handles were so good that our neighborhood giant, Joe Mussack, had Pap make the extra strong ones he had to have. Pap was a fine carpenter and the best wood chopper in the neighborhood. He doctored all the sick animals on our place and got called to help with the sick stock on neighboring farms. He grafted fruit trees, crossed varieties of plants and vines; knew cures for snake bite and ivy poisoning; and spayed, castrated, caponized and did other kinds of animal doctoring. No one had taught him these things, he just seemed always to know how.

Sometimes, however, he guessed wrong about a critter's ailments or prescribed the wrong remedy. One winter we had an epidemic of hog cholera and the animals were dying by the dozens. First they would lose their appetites, then they would have the cramps and a hoarse cough. Soon after this they would die. Pap had a fine barrow that quit eating for a day or two, and developed a bad cough. We put him in a pen by himself and waited for the inevitable.

That Saturday night in town all the farmers were talking about the cholera epidemic. Luther Talbot said that down in the Jim Linder neighborhood the farmers had cured their sick hogs with tobacco juice. Chauncey Blodgett, who never used the stuff, agreed that it ought to be good for something. Pap said little but he was taking in all the comments about the tobacco cure.

Early the next morning Pap went to work. He cut a plug of Horse Shoe into little squares and Mother boiled them for half an hour in an iron pot on the kitchen stove. As soon as the water got a good rich color he poured it into a long-necked bottle and we all went down to the sick hog. The older boys hung onto the barrow and Pap pried open his mouth and poured every bit of the mixture down the hog's throat.

As soon as the boys let him go, the hog staggered into a pile of straw, keeled over on his side and began to tremble as if he were having a chill. Pap put a horse blanket over him but he shook worse than ever. Inside of ten minutes he straightened out to full length and settled down as quiet as a stone. It was all over and the prize hog was dead, dead as a door nail, dead as Pharoah — dead from a dose of tobacco poisoning big enough to have put twenty hogs out of business.

Pap never let on like anything had gone wrong. He just turned to us and said "Well, he didn't die of cholera, anyway." And he was certainly right about that!

Then there was the horse named Shug. Shug never was healthy. He was an off-looking animal too. His feet were as big as half bushel measures and usually split badly. His hair never shed like other horses but hung in stringy wisps. He had great big ugly lumps under his belly and nearly all the hair came out of his tail. In spite of all his bad luck, however, he grew to be a big, bony horse and furnished Pap with every excuse to practice his home remedies.

When Shug was about six years old he fattened out and shed his surplus hair. Pap put him in a box stall in the barn and intended to sell him to the first person making an offer. But then Shug got sick again and began to look bad.

About the same time Pap had bought a new force pump, fifty feet of garden hose and a nozzle that could squirt water to the top of the house. One day Pap got the idea that we ought to try squirting Shug with the new equipment. After the treatment we turned poor Shug loose in the apple orchard but he just staggered behind a hay stack and collapsed.

After supper, when I started after the cows, I went past that way to see how Shug was getting along. He was lying close against the hay stack, stretched out like he was asleep. I went up and gave him a little punch, but he didn't budge a bit. He was asleep, all right, and he never woke up either. It took us all working steady 'til almost bed time to dig a hole big enough to bury him. But we finally got it done, rolled Shug in and covered him up for good and all.

Pap said we had overdone the pump treatment. But we kids never could see, for the life of us, how we could be included in the blame. Pap gave all the signals — all we did was to work the pump handle.

We didn't always come out so well with new machinery, either. Pap had bought a Minneapolis twine binder, the first in the neighborhood, and folks came for miles around to see it cut and bind the grain. Pap took a great pride in it, for it was a wonderful looking machine, almost as big as a thrasher, and cost $350. At the end of harvest that year haying was right on top of us, and Pap left that new binder out in the apple orchard for a few days before he put in it its shed. Boy-like, I had to do some tinkering with that binder.

Whenever I got a chance, and nobody was watching, I would pull down the twine in a loop about the size of a bundle, trip the trigger and turn the binding apparatus over, and watch the little thingumbob grab the twine and tie it in a chicken-head knot. I bet I did that more than a hundred times during the two or three days the binder sat there. I hid the twine I was wasting in a half caved-in old well down by the Jack barn.

I made a careful study of the cog wheels that ran along one end, and wondered just what each one had to do with the operations. Finally curiosity got the best of me, and I pulled the cotter key and slipped one of the middle cog wheels off to see whether the binder would tie a knot without it. But when I had the handles about half way over the whole thing locked itself tight and refused to go on or go back. I shook it, and wiggled it, and tried to force it, but all to no use. There it was. I had ruined it — and had Pap to deal with when he came in from the field!

The first thing I thought of was to run away. Then I decided to deny all knowledge of the happening, and stick to it. Then I remembered that Mother and one of my sisters had seen me monkeying with that binder, and had told me a time or two that I had better leave it alone. I was in an awful fix. All I could do was to wait for developments and take whatever came.

The men came in to dinner, ate, rested a while, and went back to the fields without noticing a thing. That evening they walked right past the binder, doing the chores, but never paid the least attention to it. And there stuck both handles straight up in the air. Anybody should have noticed that they didn't belong that way!

This went on for a couple of days when there came a lull in the field work and Pap called all hands to help roll the binder under its new shed, and put up the heavy door. I felt something give way in my insides, and I had the hardest kind of a time to get my breath. But I went along with the men, because I couldn't get out of it.

A mole had thrown up a little mound of fresh dirt right in the path, and the men all stopped to look at it, and that gave me a chance to get to the binder first without being noticed. There was a gunny sack lying there that twine had come in, and quick as a flash, I grabbed it up and threw it over the binder handles. That saved the day for me, I am just as sure as can be. Not a soul noticed it and in a few minutes the binder was in its shed with the big door fastened shut.

For the first time in three days I breathed easier again. The sun shone, the birds sang, food tasted better. Life was again worth living. It would be a whole year before anybody saw that binder again, and I would have all that time to get it put back together again. The exodus of the Children of Israel from Egyptian bondage couldn't have meant any more to them than this escape did to me. It wasn't the fear of a flogging so much as that sneaking feeling you have when you get caught in some kind of devilment. That was where the shoe pinched the worst. If there is any worse feeling than that I never found out what it was.

In a week or so I got a chance to slip into the shed without anyone seeing me. But it was the same old story — everything locked as tight as a drum. A few days later I got another chance, but again without any results. I suppose that the balance of that summer I made as many as forty trials and each trial ended the same way, with not a particle of progress made.

I thought about getting John Cappes to help some day when the folks were gone, but the Cappes didn't have a binder and probably he wouldn't know any more about the machine than I did. Then there was always the danger that he might forget and say something about the machine, and the secret would get out.

At last I decided to write to Minneapolis where it was made, and ask them how to fix it. But how would you describe a thing like that! After four or five times at trying to write a letter I was so confused that I didn't even know myself what I was trying to say. So I gave that up too.

During the winter I even tried a couple of times to fix that binder. But it was so cold in the shed that my hands got numb and I was forced to give up. So I had to wait for Spring.

Along late in March I tried again. But it was simply

no use. I couldn't budge the thing and I began to lose all hope.

Pretty soon it was mid-June and in three weeks' time harvest would be here again. Then the whole monstrous truth would come out and I'd really be in for it. Every time I thought about it I could feel hot flashes run all the way up and down my spine.

About that time we had a lesson at Sunday school about "The Way of the Transgressor Is Hard." The teacher laid it on pretty strong and did his level best to bring out the main points in that lesson, but he didn't half do it justice. I could have told him things on that subject he had never dreamed about.

About the first of July things began looking so black that I began to pray in earnest. I would go away off in some quiet place and plead with God to show me how to fix that confounded binder. Once I rode a mile or more into the woods to be sure I was all alone. There I bared my troubles, confessed I had done wrong, and begged for help. I tried reading the Bible to see if I could get any light but I never found a thing in there about binders, or any kind of machinery. But I did stumble onto a passage where people were told to do their praying in a closet, so I decided to try that.

That night, when everybody was sound asleep, I slid out from behind Frank, slipped down stairs and cat-footed it to the closet. I went right in and shut the door behind me. Then I got down on my knees and did some real praying. I felt sure I was going to get somewhere now, as I was following out instructions to the letter. I admitted I had done a great wrong, pleaded for mercy, and asked for light on the subject that had been bothering me so long. Then I went upstairs to bed again and had a fairly good night's sleep.

Next morning, long before getting up time, I was out at the shed, trying my hand again on fixing that binder. I set my eyes on that set of cog wheels in front, and wiggled the handles, first one way and then the other. Pretty soon my eyes fell on a trigger sort of thing that was resting against a lug. I raised the lug up, so the trigger didn't touch, and, believe it or not, the handles came free so I could turn them backward. When that lug came around again to where the trigger caught on it, I lifted it again with the same results, and in another minute or two I had the handles back where they belonged.

Then I clapped the cog wheel back in place and the binder worked just as well as it ever did.

No one knew how relieved and thankful I was. My heart filled with gratitude to God for the help He had given. It may seem a small thing for God to get interested in, but He knew that to me it was the biggest kind of case and amounted to far more than running a government or straightening out some other mess.

When we moved the binder out of its shed a week later, Frank noticed that the oil can was toppled over on its side and told me to straighten it. But I pretended not to hear him and just left it lying there. I would not have tried to change anything about that binder for the best horse in Iowa.

belle
of
cedar
and
island
chieftain

Pap pioneered in livestock breeding in our community too. Up to this time people in general thought of a cow as just a cow and let it go at that. But it wasn't hard to notice that some cows gave twice as much milk as others, and that the milk of some was richer. When it came to fattening steers for market, some fattened easily to twelve or thirteen hundred pounds while others weighed no more than half that when we sold them. Farmers talked about breeding up the stock, but for quite a spell it never amounted to anything but talk.

One day an advertisement came out in the Burlington *Gazette* about a herd of pure-bred Durham cattle somewhere over in Illinois, and offering heifer calves as low as a hundred dollars. Pap ran his finger along the lines of that piece and spelled out every word, clean to the end. Then he laid the paper down and picked up the almanac, to see what the weather was to be. After that he took up the paper again and read that piece once more, slowly and carefully. Then he got up and went to bed.

Next morning his mind was all made up. He had been the first to buy a lot of other things, so he decided to go to Illinois and buy a full bred Durham heifer. He had over two hundred dollars cash in his pocket book, and could afford to do it. Before ten o'clock he was off in the big wagon, with all the sideboards on, bound for Illinois and a heifer calf.

Several days later he came driving in with his prize calf. It was a beauty, and no mistake about it. Just weaned, and broke to lead. It had a halter on, made little so as to fit it, and when the men lifted her down to the ground, she led right off to the barn just like a horse. We had never seen anything like it.

Pap was awfully careful with that calf. She had oats, and bran, and middlings, and clover hay to eat. She was never allowed to run out in bad weather, and sometimes Pap curried her just like we did the horses. She grew up fast and by the time she was three years old she was bigger than any cow on the place, had broad level hips, hind legs about as straight as her front ones. Pap had figured that when the first calf came it would be a heifer, and then he would have two full bloods. But it wasn't, and Pap was kind of down about it.

Next day great plans were made for milking Belle Cedar, for that is what we called her. Her registered name was Belle of Cedar, but we never called her all of that, what was the use? The girls were always in the majority at our house, and as far back as I can remember, they always did the milking. So my sister Belle, being partly the same name as the new cow, claimed the right to milk her first.

But Belle Cedar had some other ideas. The first thing she did was to kick the milk bucket, stool, and sister Belle clean over backward, and give a big lunge and land with her front feet in the manger. Her eyes looked kind of walley, and she acted like she was most scared to death.

Then my brother Joe allowed he would have to milk her 'til she got broke to it, and he gathered up the tools and squatted down to commence. But he didn't even get started. Belle Cedar just snorted, and cavorted, and acted up so ugly that Joe had to back off and give it up. So the men got a rope and fastened her hind legs together so she couldn't kick, and then Joe tried his hand again. But it was worse than before.

That crazy cow reared and pitched something awful, and finally fell right over on her back with her neck bent away around sideways like it was likely to break in two. Pap ran in and cut the halter rope and eased her up, and pretty soon she rolled over on her side and got up. Her eyes were nearly all white now, her nostrils were bigger, and she shook her head like she wanted to horn somebody.

But a cow has got to be milked some way so after a while the men rigged another kind of harness that took in her front legs as well as the hind ones, and they stretched a rope from her halter up to a beam, lifted her head high so she couldn't break her neck, and went at it again. But it was no use. That purebred shorthorn cow wasn't going to be milked by anybody, and she never was. Several times afterwards we tried it again, and it always turned out just the same way, but we never carried the thing as far as the first time. So the young calf was allowed to run with its mother and get all the milk it could manage, and it was the same way with every calf she ever had.

Belle of Cedar never did come up to Pap's expectations. She had eleven calves in the ten years we had her, and two of them were twins, but there never was a heifer calf in the whole bunch. Of course, Pap was able to sell these calves to the neighbors at a good round price, and everybody around soon had herds of high grade cattle, but as far as a purebred herd was concerned, we never got it. There have to be purebred mothers to breed purebred stock.

Belle Cedar was not only an outlaw when it came to milking, but in several other ways. She was as breachy as all get out, and could jump any fence on the farm. More than a hundred times we had to round her up out of the corn fields, and two or three time she got foundered and came mighty near dying. Once she got such a dose of green corn that she was sick for months. Some of her hoofs came off, and she got to be as thin as a rail. We tried yokes, and pokes, and tieing a board over her eyes, but she got them off, somehow, and over the fences she would go. It had a bad effect on the other cattle too, and a good many of them got to be pretty breachy too. But none of them ever equalled Belle Cedar.

Finally Pap ran onto a contraption at a hardware store that was guaranteed to stop cattle from jumping fences. It was a yoke with a bow fastening around the neck, a long handle of a thing running down toward the ground, and a set of four sharp prongs held in place by a spring. These would gouge right into the animal's neck if it pushed against anything with that handle. So he bought one and put it on Belle Cedar.

It worked fine. Several times I saw her go up to the rail fence around the corn field and make ready to jump over. But when that handle caught under the rails she would get a rousing jab in the neck, then would back off and shake her head, and look pretty foolish. She wore that new fangled yoke several weeks and never jumped a fence once.

But one day, when I was prowling around down

in the pasture, I ran onto Belle Cedar lying on her side down by the creek bank, and breathing like a person that snores. I went up close to see what was the matter and discovered that the yoke bow which went around her neck was imbedded in the flesh as much as three or four inches. I went for help as fast as I could. Pap and the other boys hurried down there and tried with all their mights to get that yoke off. But it was too tight, so Pap sent for a handsaw to saw it off. But before the saw got there Belle Cedar was dead. That yoke always was pretty small for a cow with as heavy a neck as hers, and it had chafed her neck, Pap said, and started a swelling, and had just kept on until the flesh on her neck had fairly covered the yoke. She had just naturally choked to death.

All in all, Belle Cedar was pretty much of a failure, and that hindered Pap's efforts at building up a pure-bred herd of Durham cattle. But he wasn't discouraged. In fact you couldn't tell that he even felt sorry about anything like this and I reckon that was the reason he lived to be ninety-four.

It wasn't long 'til Pap had a new idea — the raising of fine horses. Again he went to Illinois, this time to John Greenwood's farm at Alexis, and brought home a fine two year old Clydesdale stallion named Island Chieftain. This time, however, he invested a cool thousand dollars.

Island Chieftain was light bay in color, had a mane that came half way down to his knees and had feet that were nearly as big as half bushel measures. When he was full grown he weighed two thousand pounds. Chief was a great success in every way so that Pap got a lot of satisfaction caring for him. Chief was as gentle as a dog and anybody could ride him, if they were in no hurry.

We never went in for fast horses, but we did have a young horse that was hard to beat in a race. We called him "Taller," which was our word for tallow. I don't know to this day why we ever came to call him that. Frank was fifteen or sixteen years old about that time, and he named a good many things around the place. Some of the names he thought up were curious ones, too. He had a pony named *Loafer* which, in spite of his name, was the spryest, handiest little horse you ever saw.

Frank also named the unfortunate Shug and conferred such names as *Knickerbocker* and *Grindstaff* on the other horses. Edith, my youngest sister, once named a calf *Pete Beat Easter,* since the calf was born the day before Easter.

I ran a good many races with Taller and mighty seldom found a common plug which could outrun him. We never raced for money, just for sport. But we put as much enthusiasm into it as if there was big money at stake.

Down in the Pleasant Grove neighborhood an old man named Jack Smith owned a big farm of several hundred acres. He and his three sons raised racing horses and always went to all the fairs to run their horses. We heard that Old Jack, as he was called, made

pots of money at it. Our neighborhood didn't reach
that far as to school districts, swapping work at thrashing time or anything like that, so we seldom saw the
Smith boys. But once in a while they would ride some
of their colts up to Yarmouth, looking for a race with
our work horses.

One Saturday afternoon during a baseball game between Yarmouth and Tamytown, the Smith boys came
riding in. They stood around making fun of our horses
during the game and challenged any of us to a race as
soon as it was finished.

None of us ever raced horses for money so the Smith
boys got ready to ride off. But Dave Michaels agreed
at the last minute to bet a dollar that they didn't have
a horse which could run a quarter of a mile while my
Taller ran sixty rods. The Smith boys tried to get the
distance Taller must run boosted to sixty-five rods, but
Dave wouldn't bet that way. Finally after a lot of argu-
ing and cussing the brothers agreed to the terms, so the
men measured off the distances. At the crack of the
pistol we were off with Taller running better than he
had ever run before.

But I was hardly started when the Smith boy shot
past me. Honestly, it seemed like I was almost standing
still. I never realized before what a fast animal a
thoroughbred racing horse is. I never finished the
course, for the Smith horse was a hundred yards ahead
of me and kicking up a fog of dust. Dave handed over
his dollar and the Smith boys rode off feeling mighty
cocky. After that I never pitted my horse against any-

thing but work horses, and I generally could beat them as handily as that thoroughbred had whipped us.

Our community also had some fine hunting dogs. Henry Rawhert brought a blooded setter with him that was a surprise to the neighborhood with its smart setting and retrieving. Several of the men couldn't rest until they had scraped up money somehow to buy themselves good hunting dogs, too. Soon half of the farmers owned good dogs that would work prairie chicken, quail, and other wild game. Then people felt they had to buy better guns and hunting equipment, so they were pretty well outfitted.

We had a neighbor living about three miles west of us who always wore a white paper collar and drove a spanking team of high stepping trotters hitched to a light buggy. His name was Milt Wise and he bought cattle and hogs for market.

Milt always carried a wad of paper money big enough to choke a cow and he put on the dog generally. He operated a good-sized farm and had his house fixed up with all the latest conveniences. All of us believed Wise was rich and probably was planning to buy out all his smaller neighbors someday.

He smoked expensive cigars all the time, had ivory rings all over his harness and carried a buggy whip that must have cost at least a dollar. He took a particular pleasure in driving up and down the roads as fast as his team could trot — passing every other buggy and wagon.

There was a new bridge across a big creek east of

us which had a sign on it reading: "Five Dollars Fine for Driving Over This Bridge Faster Than a Walk."

At the opening of this new bridge the supervisors, the town clerk, the justice of the peace and many others were gathered for the occasion. Then Wise came driving past and raced right out on that bridge in a full trot.

One of the supervisors stopped Wise and told him that he was breaking the law, and that he owed the county a five dollar fine for doing it. Wise said that was all right and was a good rule. Then he flicked the ashes off his cigar, hauled out his wad of greenbacks, peeled off a ten dollar bill and handed it to the supervisor with the remark that he wanted no change since he was coming back that way in an hour and wanted to trot his horses over the bridge again. That was his way. He seemed to be made of money and didn't care a hoot about expenses.

A year or two later the sheriff closed down on Wise and levied on some of his property to satisfy a claim against him. That set off a whole chain of events, and the upshot of it was that he lost everything he had in the world. It came out at last that Wise never did have anything, but was just one of these high flyers who can make a go of living on borrowed money and get away with it for a considerable spell. But everybody liked Wise, and a lot of folks thought he was the finest man in the school district.

Pap was about as far from a fourflusher as anybody could be. He was absolutely on the up and up, and nobody ever lost anything dealing with him. He never went into debt a dollar in his life. If he didn't have the cash to pay in full he just didn't buy, that was all. It was his way and nobody was ever able to change him. He nearly always carried quite a wad of money in his pockets, and never stood back for anybody when it came to buying something new and being the first one to have it.

I will never forget how proud we all were when he came home from Burlington with a John Glazeby top buggy that cost a hundred and seventy-five dollars. It was a one horse buggy and our big rangy sorrel mare, Fox, could make the wheels fairly hum along the road. But nobody but Pap ever got to drive that buggy. Once in a while he and Mother would take it to drive over to New London — ten miles away — to church, but mostly that blessed buggy sat in a barn stall covered up with a canvas for a month or two before he took a notion to go some place else.

Once he took me along twenty-five miles to Burlington to pay our taxes. We started right after dinner and drove to Flint Creek, about five miles from Burlington, where we stayed all night.

Pap took along feed for Fox so he unhitched her and tied her to a tree while we ate the lunch Mother had fixed for us. Then we slept in the buggy. But it was such a wonderful place among the big trees beside a dashing creek and so close to the big town that I didn't fall asleep until nearly morning. We were wakened by roosters crowing. Not two rods away was

Yankee Jack and his huckster wagon, all cluttered up with chicken coops. He was stopping there too and aiming to get to town for the early market.

It was my first trip to our county seat town. What a wonderful sight it was to ride down Sunny Side Avenue in that great city and see the fine houses and barns. Pap told me some of the houses even had electric lights, running water to wash and swim in, and handles in the middle of doors which Pap said were to ring a bell when we wanted in. The front yards were as big as good sized barn lots, all mowed smooth as could be. Gee, but it was thrilling!

We didn't drive down the main streets, for they had street cars which frightened the horses, and Pap refused to take any chance of smashing up the buggy. When we finally got to the main part of town where the stores were we found hundreds of people hurrying about, with about as many going one way as another. Nearly everybody was dressed up, a lot of them wore white collars, and some of them carried canes.

For the life of me I could not figure out how anybody could find his way around, or even find his way home. There were hundreds of streets and alleys and they all looked alike to me. Down at the foot of Jefferson street lay the great Mississippi River, half a mile wide and, I supposed, hundreds of feet deep. Two or three big steam boats were tied at the bank while a lot of Negroes loaded and unloaded the cargoes as fast as they could. Nearly half the river was covered with timber rafts, some nearly half a mile long. One was tied to the bank with big ropes while men were fishing out lumber and logs to load them on wagons. Some of these men stood waist deep in the water to work. But they didn't seem to mind it at all.

Farther down the river were three or four great sawmills, whizzing and whirring and making the sawdust fly. Great log rafts which had been floated down from the northern pine forests were tied to the banks. From these rafts the logs were jerked out of the water and onto the sawmill carriers by some kind of machinery. Then the carrier would go rolling up against the great saw with much whining and grumbling but soon another pine board would flop down. Pap said they just kept that up day and night, but what they ever did with all that lumber I couldn't cipher out.

I never expect to spend another day as full of wonders as that one was. We ate dinner at Runge's restaurant with its looking glass reaching across the whole side of the room, its silver knives, forks and spoons and its tumblers as thin as paper. Paper napkins to fix under our chins and a big overhead fan to keep us cool while we ate seemed to me to make Runge's the finest place in the world.

After dinner Pap went to Carpenter's Jewelry Store to get the correct time and set his watch. Then after looking into the windows of some of the big stores we got Fox and the precious buggy to head for home. By four o'clock we were out to Flint Creek, in another hour we reached Dodgeville and were well on the way home.

By this time the excitement was over and the first

thing I knew I bumped over against Pap, sleepy as a puppy. He fixed me in the corner of the seat with my head against the bows. There I slept like a log for a long time. When finally I woke up deep in the night Pap was fast asleep also. Fox was trotting along the way home like she knew where she was going so I dropped off again and did not wake up until the buggy was stopped and Fox was standing with her head over our barn lot gate. I woke Pap up, we unhitched the horse and slept in some hay until the men came out to do the morning chores.

For days I could talk or think of nothing but that wonderful trip. There may have been places that beat that county seat, but the boy never lived whose heart was more nearly filled with delights than mine was after that first trip to Burlington, city of marvelous sights and sounds.

springtime

on

old

orchard

farm

While every part of the year was exciting on the farm, spring was the finest of all. It was such a big change from winter, with everything frozen up, and nothing stirring much except the livestock. But when spring set in everything seemed to come to life, the air filled up with bugs and insects, birds came surging back from the South, while wild geese and ducks, on their trip to the North, just filled the ponds and lakes all around us.

Iowa was a young state and there was lots of water on the surface of the ground. Every section of land had a pond or two, and out west of our place three or four miles lay Canaan Flats, a wide stretch of perfectly level land, wet and soggy — just the kind of a place wild fowls were looking for. We herded the cattle in there sometimes in summer, when the pastures would get too short, and the horse we were riding would sink in halfway to his knees. It was mostly blue stem and ramrod that grew there, and the cattle didn't care so very much about it. But they would eat it after they got good and hungry.

Early in the spring we always finished up the wood pile. It was hard to keep your mind on your work when wild geese and ducks were flying over and lighting in the fields to feed. We could look off any direction and see six or seven great flocks, some of them several hundred, either soaring away up high on their way north, or circling around getting ready to land. Then all at once a great big flock of wild geese came down in a wheat field not forty rods away. They looked as big as turkeys sitting there right out in the open, only five rods from the hedge fence.

If Pap was at home we went and told him, and he was apt to say, "Well, finish up your work, and do the chores, then you can go and try your hand." But if Pap was gone to Yarmouth, we would get out Old Dalsey and the musket right away and start out. Generally it was a good deal farther than we supposed, because geese are so big they look closer than they really are.

When we peeped through the hedge fence at those geese pottering around in the young wheat right before our eyes, our hearts would palpitate and our legs just tremble. The question was to get close enough to shoot. Could we do it without scaring them away? For sure, it was an exciting time.

When we got up to within a hundred yards we took another look, and there they were, bigger than ever — some feeding, some just sitting around unconcerned, and some with their eyes peeled on the lookout for danger.

But we crawled closer on our hands and knees, over ground soaked with water, and with hedge thorns once in a while sticking out of the dead grass. The musket was only good for about forty yards, but Old Dalsey, which was a rifle, would bring them down at two hundred yards if you could hold her steady. But we wanted one goose for the musket and one for Old Dalsey. So we crawled a little closer.

Only fifty yards now from that wonderful flock of wild geese! We could see the stripes on their necks, and hear them jabbering with one another. Then we scootched down a little closer to the ground, and inched along, right on our bellies for another rod or two.

Then a terrible thing happened. There was a wild flapping of wings and such a honking as you never heard and away went that whole flock of three or four hundred geese. We raised up and banged away with both guns. But the geese, although they looked as big as fanning mills, were too far away for the musket, and we couldn't hit anything on the wing with a rifle anyhow. There we stood, with our mouths open, and watched those blessed geese 'til they went out of sight behind Fred Smith's hill. Then we went back to our wood chopping again.

Nobody had any very good guns in those days, and the two we had were no better than the rest. We had not yet learned about decoys, blinds, or any other fine points of hunting. As a result we generally didn't get a thing, as far as geese and ducks were concerned. But we got to shoot at them, and that was worth a lot. We always figured that we would get them the next time.

We soon learned that a wild goose must appear to be only two or three rods away to really be close enough to shoot. But it was mighty hard for a boy to hold his fire while those great birds approached. Something always told us to shoot and usually we did. We also learned not to shoot while the birds were headed toward us. When we did, the shot just rattled off their feathers unless we were lucky enough to hit their heads or necks. When we were able to hold back until they had passed over, we had a better chance to get a bird.

Sometimes we had good luck. I shall never forget a time when Jodie Williams, an orphan living with us at the time, and I went over to the lake to take a shot at some butter ducks we had seen light in a round pond behind a grove of willow bushes. We sure did slay them that time.

A stray dog had been making his home with us for two or three weeks. He was black as a coal and deaf as a post. He had long wavy hair, dangling ears and web feet like a duck. Chauncey Blodgett allowed he was a spaniel. The dog was tickled to death when we threw sticks into the water so he could dive in and bring them out. He would do that all day, if anybody would keep throwing the sticks. We named him Heck. So Heck went along with us that day after the butter ducks.

Jodie and I slipped along behind the willows until we were only forty feet from the pond, there we peeped through a little opening and saw almost a hundred of the prettiest little wild ducks, splashing water, and chasing one another around. Jodie poked the old musket through some twigs, took a good rest over a chunk that was lying there, and let drive. There was a terrible fluttering of wings and squawking, as the ducks scrambled out of there, and we popped through the thicket to see what we had.

Heck went right into the pond and began bringing out the ducks. He kept it up, without stopping to rest, until he had ten of them at our feet. He never even shook himself until he was all through, but then he splashed about a gallon of water all over us. But what did we care? We had a wonderful string of ducks to take to the house and show the folks, and nothing else counted.

On the way home we had an experience that proved just how ignorant a young boy can be. Heck was out ahead of us when suddenly he stopped dead still and stared into a clump of little bushes. There he stood, not moving a muscle until we passed him. Even then he didn't show any sign of following us. We called him but he didn't pay any attention. Then we walked on hoping he would follow, but Heck just stood his ground and wouldn't budge.

Jodie and I couldn't understand what had happened to that dog. He was a smart dog but he was acting mighty funny. I thought maybe the water had dazed him but Jodie was afraid he had gone mad. We didn't know what to do and were about ready to break and run when the dog lunged into the bushes, leaping and snapping in all directions as a big covey of quail flew out. Heck had tried to tell us about those birds, for he was a setter as well as a retriever. It was a case of a dog knowing more than two boys. Even that was not saying too much for the dog.

Once I shot a low flying goose just as twilight was closing in. She didn't fall immediately but I saw her sag down when I shot and I knew the bird was badly hit. I watched her mighty close but it was pretty dark. She dropped out of sight when she was even with the tops of the cornstalks so I ran over as fast as I could to search in the dark, but I couldn't find a trace of her. Then I went home and did the chores. After supper I took a lantern and Frank and I searched up and down every corn row, but had no luck, even though we kept looking until nine o'clock.

Next morning just as daylight came out of the East I was out again searching that cornfield. Finally I got up on the rail fence, on the far side, and looked across a pasture. I could see a black looking object away over toward the other side, so I ran over there to see. It was my goose, or what was left of her. But the coyotes had beaten me there. All that was left was a few bones and feathers. It was a cruel blow for that was my first wild goose. But what a night I had made for the coyotes!

Many other kinds of water birds passed through every spring. Plover, snipes, rails, curlews, loons, cranes, and the like came by the thousands. And what wonderful flyers the sand hill cranes were. They came late in the spring, after the grass was green, and hardly ever lit in our parts. Usually they flew as much as half a mile high, circling all the time in kind of long sweeps, in no hurry at all. They made a guttural kind of sound not a bit like any other bird, and you could hear them for some time before they came in sight. We used to lie on our backs, shade our eyes with our hands, and look all over the sky for them. Finally, away off yonder, looking not much bigger than humming birds, we could see a big flock of cranes circling around and coming over. Like as not it would be ten or fifteen minutes before they passed over us and went out of sight.

Dick Peckham had a 32 Winchester which he always claimed would bring down a sand hill crane, no matter how high he was flying. Dick said it would shoot two miles on the level, so why not up in the air? We always thought he was stretching it a little, but he said, "Wait and see, you don't understand a regular breech loader."

Not long afterward, when we were in the pasture

drowning out ground squirrels, Dick came by with his famous rifle. He said he wouldn't waste his high priced ammunition on such things as ground squirrels, but if we could find a ground hog or a coyote he would show us something about how a real rifle could shoot. But just then a big flock of cranes came circling over so Dick emptied his gun at them. First, he tried the leader, with three or four shots, then he fired a little farther back into the flock. The rest of the cartridges he fired sort of all over doing his level best to bring down a crane.

But as far as we could see he didn't disturb them at all. They didn't seem to even hear the shots, and didn't pay the slightest attention. They circled around as lazy as you please and finally flew out of sight. Dick said he didn't have the regular kind of cartridges made for his rifle, and that's why he didn't have any better luck. So he shot a few ground squirrels for us, then made out that he had work to do and went on home.

Once in a big field by the Carter place we saw a flock of cranes on the ground about eighty rods away. They looked bigger than turkeys, with necks even longer. I always wondered how these big birds could fly as far as they did without stopping to rest. They must have been "fearfully and wonderfully made," as our teacher said. A lot of things are, if you stop to think about it.

In the spring the first clap of thunder brought out the frogs. It was a sure sign of spring when along in the evening they began to sing to beat anything. In the creek there were swarms of minnows and suckers as well as some pretty fair sized bullheads. It surely was fun to fish off the edge of our bridge in that clear, four-foot pool under the big bridge while our feet dangled down. We cut our poles in a willow thicket, used common store twine for string and a bent pin for a hook. The fish would jerk the cork almost as soon as it hit the water and a pint of fishworms wouldn't last an hour. Of course, lots of fish bit that we never caught, for a pin hook had no barb on it. Unless we jerked the line at exactly the right moment, the fish was gone. But we caught a good many bullheads, some good sized redhorse, and sometimes a sucker or two.

Once when we got caught in a heavy rain storm while fishing we crawled under the bridge where a shelf stuck out. But we forgot to think that a bridge with a plank floor wouldn't turn water. Water poured down through the cracks, washing all the dirt down with it to leave us the dirtiest looking brats in the neighborhood when we finally crawled out. We were ashamed to go to the house so we took off our clothes, washed them in the creek and went swimming while they dried on the fence. There may have been sports which were more fun than that kind of fishing, but we never found them. It was good enough for me.

We were deathly afraid of snakes. This was partly because we always went barefooted and partly because of the big stories people told about rattlers. Once in a great while, of course, somebody ran across a rattler, but he was really a scarce snake. We ran onto lots of garter snakes, as harmless as flies, but we jumped back when we saw them just the same. But we always kept clear of the blue racer. He was a deep blue color, lived in the grass and was generally found in wet or low places. He was sure a fast runner. The ones I saw were going the other way just as fast as they could streak, then would disappear in the grass. I never could understand why a poisonous snake, as we thought the blue racer to be, would always run the other way as fast as he could when we ran across him. I always expected the next one to run up my britches leg and bite me a time or two before I could strip off my clothes.

Pierkses two boys said that down in their pasture they saw a blue racer run right up a horse's leg, bite him three or four times on the back and then jump off. The horse, they claimed, died that very night with both eyes swollen shut and his tongue hanging out. They said more than a thousand blue racers lived on their farm. We stayed off the Pierkses farm after that. And they had some of the best eating apples in the country!

Springtime brought big rains that made the creek come clear up. That gave us the chance for some of the grandest adventures that boys ever had. When there was a freshet, we dragged an old horse trough down the hill to use as a boat. Then we poled it down to the lower flood gate. After this we would walk along the slippery bank, pulling our craft back to the starting place to do it all over again. We always pretended we were savages on headhunting expeditions in the jungle so we did all this without a stitch of clothes on. When our skin peeled a few days later from sunburn we really looked a good deal like savages. And we felt like them too.

One thing that never failed us when we were out for blood on these trips was that curious crab-like creature we called the crawdad. They were built like lobsters with the meanest kind of pinchers for hands, and carried their young wrapped up under their flat tails. They crawled forward on land but swam backward in the water. At the time of a freshet we could find them by the dozens at the mouth of every little draw that emptied into the creek.

We used to fasten our boat at these crawdad stations and make raids on them. We called them the "Americans" and were out to capture them dead or alive. It wasn't very hard to do, but we made out that it was dangerous business. We convinced ourselves that they were poisonous like blue racer snakes and that they could pinch us to death if they ever got held of us. On one trip we captured more than a bushel of these crawdads. It was a little awkward, without any clothes on, to find a good place to ride in the boat with several hundred crawling monsters, every one equipped with poisonous fangs and anxious to deal us a paralyzing blow. But we managed to get along and finally arrived at the lower floodgate with our whole cargo.

What to do with them was then the question. When we took a vote on it, the majority was in favor of cutting their heads off, but we had only one pocket knife in the crowd, and it was half a mile up the creek in Frank's britches pocket, so we smashed a few of them as a warning to the rest, and let it go at that. Then we hauled the boat out on the bank, and turned it upside down, while that whole ugly swarm of "Americans" scrambled down the bank into the water. We waited to see whether any of them would come out again to fight, but none of them showed up. So we wrote a warning on the floodgate with a piece of soapstone, and decided to explore farther down the creek.

We pried the floodgate open a couple of feet and finally got the horse-trough through. Then we got aboard and went sailing through Schomp's field without permission. We pushed around great bends and under overhanging trees as reckless as you please. Now and then we came to a place where another creek emptied in and then our creek would be a lot wider and deeper.

It was the bulliest kind of sport. Once in sailing around a sharp bend our boat started spinning and one end banged into the bank. Then the other end swung around with the current to hit the other bank and stop dead in the water. Pretty soon the driftwood and rubbish commenced gathering and backed up the water so it was nearly a foot deeper on the upper side of our boat. But just about the time we decided to abandon ship she broke loose so away we went again with driftwood, rubbish and all. After that we were pretty careful about how we sailed around the bends.

We got so wrapped up in this thing that we went right under a big wagon bridge without caring a cent. Pretty soon we passed another creek mouth which brought in even more water — covered with foam and rubbish. We sailed through a big willow grove that none of us could remember and once we passed in plain sight of a house, but they didn't seem to notice us. We talked a little about going right on around the world, but since we didn't have even a rag of clothes on that was out of the question. So we gave it up.

Frank said he believed we were near the Peckham farm. This scared us, for Peckham was a mighty strange sort of man who might shoot us, likely as not. So we crawled out on the muddy bank to look around. We were more than a mile below the big bridge we had sailed under, and our clothes were at least half a mile above that. We tried poling the boat, but the current was too swift for that. We couldn't even hold our own — the water was coming so fast. Then we started to wade along the edge of the water and tried to keep out of sight under the bank. But every little ways the bank got so steep we finally made up our minds to stay out and beat it up the bank as fast as we could.

In a little while the chuckle of a wagon made us realize that we were below the main road and would have to get across it somehow to get back to our clothes. We made a shelter out of grass and weeds to keep the sun off and waited for a chance when no one was going past. When we did make the break we ran right into Mrs. Manson, who was on her way home from the post office. She sassed us good, saying we ought to be ashamed of ourselves. But we already were. She didn't have to tell us.

Springtime also brought lettuce, onions, dandelion greens, gooseberries, and wild strawberries. Was there ever anything as good as wild strawberries? Pie plant pie was another mighty good thing to eat. But we never could eat more than three or four pieces without getting sick. Ripe currents were not so bad either. And apples were good to eat as soon as the seeds showed up. But green plums were the bunk, believe me. We learned to wait until they were ripe. In those days there was no such thing as buying any of these fine articles in any of the stores. We had to raise them ourselves. And Mother's garden was certainly a Godsend after a long winter of pickled pork, sauerkraut, and sorghum molasses. Not that these things were not good food. But we got tired of them after a few months and wanted a change.

Our Easter celebration also was one of the events of springtime. We kids gathered all the eggs we could find and hid them in the oats bin, the granary, the salt barrel, or any other place we thought of. It was a lot of fun to hear Mother complain about the hens not laying any eggs like they ought to. We thought we were fooling her, but she was fooling us, and knew all the time what was going on.

Then on Easter morning we would come lugging in eggs by the pailful. Some Easters we had saved up as much as a hundred dozen. And how Mother would carry on about the way we had kept her in the dark about it all, and how she had been laying it all onto the poor hens. For breakfast we wouldn't have a thing but eggs. She would fry a skilletful, boil three or four dozen, scramble a big dishful, and have the table all dressed up with colored eggs made by wrapping calico around them and boiling them in water. Each one tried to see who could eat the most, and it was generally Pap who won. One Easter he ate seventeen, and we decided there wasn't any use to try to beat that.

Watermelons, muskmelons, green corn, peaches, plums, fresh mutton, catfish, once in a while a beef steak, fresh pork heart, spareribs and liver at butchering time, homemade bread, home churned butter, fresh buttermilk, cottage cheese, spiced apples, a dozen kinds of preserves, no end of canned pickles — nobody ever fared better or had any better time than we did on Old Orchard Farm.

the good old summertime

Though Pap's formal education was limited, he was
smart enough at setting up schemes to get work out of
his boys. With every nasty little job that ever came along
he would always say something to make it look easy.

One of many unknown and carefully guarded
boons Pap often proposed to bestow on us after a tough
job was finished was to "starch our pants and go and

hear the bob whites holler." We never got to do it, but we just busted to find out what it meant and to this day I get a certain thrill out of the bare mention of starching my pants to go hear the bob whites holler.

One of the hottest and meanest jobs we had to do was mowing weeds along the fence rows. On a two hundred acre farm divided into forty and twenty acre fields there was a considerable stretch of fence rows. It seems to me now that we must have had nearly four miles of plank, rail, hedge and wire fence on Old Orchard Farm. But at weed mowing time during the dog days of August it seemed we had at least a hundred miles.

We always tackled the fence rows when the weather was as hot as it ever gets. Between the tall corn and the hedge fences lay a five or six foot strip of every kind of stinking weed you ever read about. Not a breath of air could get in and the sun beat down on our heads like fury.

We used a short bladed scythe we called the "Armstrong Reaper." First we swung to the right and then to the left, with all our strength slashing into the weeds to a depth of six or seven inches. Every little while we would strike a regular sockdolager of a weed that the scythe couldn't cut and we were forced to pull it up by hand. On top of this, about every third lick we would run the point of the blade into the ground. It was work for a horse. A dozen strokes made us sweat all over and in a little bit we just had to head for the shade in the cornfield and rest.

Pollen from the corn and surrounding weeds stuck on our sweaty faces and necks so that we were as yellow as pumpkins. It itched like the dickens, but when we tried to wipe it off with a bandana handkerchief it chafed the skin all the more.

About every thirty minutes we got so thirsty we'd walk back to the water jug sitting in the weeds and sheltered from the sun. But it was a pretty poor drink, for it was usually about as warm as dishwater. It was wet, however, and that always helped. Sometimes we walked a half mile to the house or to the Cappeses to get a cool drink. And it was worth the walk, too.

Pap used strategy to get us out to cut these weeds. He always said that if we cut all the weeds during the dog days in August, they would not be there the following year. So we yanked that old scythe through those blessed weeds convinced that this was the last time we would ever have to do it. And it was, at least as far as those particular weeds were concerned. But a new crop always appeared the next year, calling for another ten days of mean and dirty work.

Corn husking always brought out another of Pap's plans for speeding up our work. Two or three of us would be on each side of the wagon and Pap would work on the down row. He was always able to find all the corn on his own row, gather up what the horses and wagon knocked off, and find every nubbin we left on the rows behind us. Late in the afternoon there was always a let down so Pap would sing out, "Here we go for cider." That meant that the sooner we husked to the end of the field the quicker we could get to the cider barrel. It always worked too. At other seasons of the year it would be "going for gravy," or "going for sausage," or whatever else came into his mind.

But life on the farm was more than ornery work and hardships. There was always enough work to keep us busy, of course, but along with the chores there were pleasant and funny experiences that relieved the monotony.

Summer brought wonderful things to Old Orchard Farm. 'Way back when the first few peeping blades of green grass appeared, we figured it was time to shuck our boots and go barefoot. There was something mighty fine about turning your bare feet out onto the fresh warm earth for a sweet summer outing. At first we had to be careful because our feet were tender from having been shut up so long. But they toughened up pretty fast and by midsummer they got so calloused that we could run anywhere — over rocks, stubble or even hedgethorns. But we never learned any way to keep from getting hurt by the saw grass that grew down along the lake. That pesky stuff would grab right onto your bare legs and scratch worse than any cat. It would burn and itch and scratching it only made matters worse.

We had a lot of fun running barefoot along the dusty lanes, kicking up great clouds of dust which floated off over the fences. And what bliss it was on a hot day to wade knee deep in the cool creek with its swift water rippling over the white pebbles.

But what a job it was to wash your dirty feet at bedtime! With feet all banged up, the bark knocked off ankle bones and only half cured, with little cracks all over the top of your feet and maybe a thorn buried in your heel, and with your legs scarred by saw grass, washing was an awful job. Mother sometimes made a short down pallet for us so that our feet could stick out, then would let us go to bed without washing them. We always appreciated that!

In early summer we got lots of fun out of hunting goose eggs among the drifts in the willow grove in the old lake bottom. Geese have a way of hiding their nests which you have to know about. An old goose will make her nest in a spot where small sticks and loose rubbish can be found. After she has laid an egg she covers the nest, doing such a good job that the place looks almost exactly like it did in the first place.

But to one who knows about geese it is different. The place where the nest is looks smoother and in damp weather looks dryer. It was fun to take off these sticks and rubbish to uncover a nest full of great white eggs. Since we never ate any of the eggs we would cover them again and go on searching for another nest. But when the old goose settled on her nest to hatch out some goslings we had to be careful. She was as sassy as could be, wouldn't budge an inch for anybody and could bite and beat fiercely with her wings.

One time four or five of us were prowling around in the grove doing nothing in particular, barefooted and as carefree as could be. I stepped over a pile of driftwood and set my foot down right alongside a stray nest where an old goose was setting. Before I realized what had happened there was a terrible pain in the lower part of my leg, a sharp hissing sound struck up and I was getting whipped around the legs by the wings of an excited goose. Then with her jagged little teeth she nabbed the big tendon that runs up from the heel. Two other boys ran up to rescue me or I would have been scared to death. That goose bite turned black and blue over night and bothered me for about a week. We learned that we couldn't be too careful if there were any nests around.

We had the grandest apple orchard you ever saw. It lay on the south slope west of the barn and had at least a hundred trees with green grass under them. When that apple orchard was in full bloom in the spring it was one of the prettiest sights of the year.

Birds lived there by the hundreds. Blackbirds, robins, thrushes, doves and flickers came there to build their nests. The flickers pecked holes in dead limbs and nested there, but the other birds used the crotches of the trees to build out where it was cool. Blackbirds and robins made some nests nearly as big as a man's hat by weaving together pieces of old rags, sticks, twigs and a little of everything they could find. Then they lined them with mud carried a mouthful at a time from the lake nearly a quarter of a mile away, and finished them with feathers to make the nest soft and comfortable. But doves were poor at it, for they only chucked a few sticks in a crotch to keep the eggs from rolling out and let it go at that. They must have had something more important to do than building nests.

We had names for most of our apple trees. I still remember the Rich tree, the Cin tree, the John D. tree, the Skin-a-cat tree, the Corner tree, the Hockey tree, the Stomach-ache tree, the Sweet tree — and perhaps forty others. All of these names meant something and stuck to the trees just like people's names.

Blossoms and blooms, birds and bees, rabbits and garter snakes, tumble bugs and hen's nests, green and ripe apples, fine places to climb and limbs to swing on, the wheat granary by the gate and the hay stack down at the lower end — all these showed us a wonderful time every day we went in.

In the evenings Pap used to turn the horses loose in the apple orchard to keep the grass mowed short. For years an old "A" harrow sat up-ended against a tree in the edge of the orchard. Behind it the grass was always a foot high. Once a work horse named Buckskin ran his head through the frame of the harrow in an effort to get at the tall grass. When he tried to straighten up he pushed his head into the fork of the harrow forming the "A."

Buckskin was so scared that he threw his head up high. This caused the harrow to slip down over his neck and stabbed the teeth into his breast. He tried to back out of the trap, then he tried to turn around, and finally he lost his reason entirely and fell in a heap with the harrow on top of him. The whole family ran to the rescue with the men trying every way to do something. But nothing worked. Then Buckskin jumped to his feet, gave a blood chilling squeal and rushed about aimlessly, first one direction and then another. He ran into a tree and nearly butted his brains out, he broke through the barn lot fence and finally fell in a tangled heap by the water trough.

The men got a rope and tied the poor horse's legs to keep him from killing himself while they cut the harrow in half. We all thought that would be the end of Buckskin, but he fooled us. Apparently he didn't wear the name for nothing. Outside of a few scratches he wasn't hurt a bit. He was a tough critter.

One spring while the men were sowing oats it was a fool steer that caused the trouble. Pap always broadcast the small grain by hand, using a sow-sack strapped over his shoulder. The supply stations for the seed were located in the middle and at both ends of the field with salt barrels serving for containers. One afternoon when the oats supply was nearly gone in the barrels, a three year old steer poked his head in for a mouthful of oats. But when he went to take his head out the barrel caught on his horns. The steer threw his head wildly into the air trying to toss off the barrel. The loose oats then came tumbling down into his eyes and nostrils. With his head in the barrel he was blind as a bat and the more he thought about it the more frightened he got.

Then he started to run across the field with his tail high. Pap and the boys cut for the fence for safety, for the steer was charging in every direction. After a little he set off toward the west at full speed — soon coming to a dry ten-foot ditch which he plunged into at full tilt. The boys hurried over, supposing the steer had broken his neck. Before they got half way, however, the steer came crawling out of the ditch with a lot of wooden hoops dangling around his neck. He had hit the bottom of the ditch hard enough to break the salt barrel into a thousand pieces, but he wasn't hurt a bit.

A runaway team of horses is as bad as anything on a farm. Everybody who ever lived in the country knows what a runaway is, but will agree that it is something worth seeing, too.

Work horses, harnessed or saddled, are as gentle as little lambs, as a rule, as long as they think you have them in hand. But remove your hand, let the horse think he is free, and there is a runaway right there. Maybe it is no more than laying down the lines a moment or relaxing control in any way and a spirited team will run away.

And a runaway horse just goes crazy. He runs at top speed and never cares what he runs into. He will run over anything that happens to be in his path, break through fences, jump over ditches, and has been known to crash right into a stone fence and break his fool neck. A genuine runaway is surely a sight.

During my years on the farm I was mixed up in several runaways. Once the lines slipped off the dashboard of a lumber wagon when I turned around to slide a post down. Before I knew what had happened, away went that team at breakneck speed with the lines dragging underneath the wagon. I was as helpless as a baby.

Nobody can imagine, unless he has had a similar experience, what a wild ride that was — over rough ground, with no springs of any kind, and the wagon bouncing two or three feet high at a bounce. It was mighty lucky for me that the team got pretty well winded before they reached the barn yard, and came to an abrupt but harmless stop at the gate. I got off alive, but about scared to death, and my hair stood on end for a good while.

Another time I got off the seat of a riding plow to go to the fence row for a drink of water. Just as I lifted the jug to my lips the three plow horses were frightened by something and away they went. As they gained speed the beam of the plow came down and the share gouged into the ground. How the dirt did boil! And those fool horses just seemed to put on more power and heaved into their collars with all the strength they had. Pretty soon the beam lifted and there was a fresh spurt of speed. Then down went the beam again and up went another stream of dirt five or six feet high.

They kept that up all the way across the field and never paid the slightest attention to the wire fence. They plunged right into it, full speed, and pulled out all the staples for a hundred yards. All three of the horses fell in a tangled heap of barbed wire. After floundering for awhile they calmed down and lay there as meek as kittens.

I ran to the house as fast as I could to bring Pap out to help. Together we cut wires and harness all to pieces before we could get those horses on their feet. Strange as it may seem, none of them was hurt. They were scratched up some, but there were no broken bones or deep cuts. But the fence, the harness and the plow were a mess.

With a team of mules it was different. Mules were still more likely to run away than horses, but a runaway mule team was more of a joke than a calamity. A mule is either too lazy to put up a real thriller or he has too much sense to take the risk of getting killed. As a rule, a runaway mule team will never get beyond inter-mediate gear and will come to a safe and sane stop within two hundred yards with no harm done. Old Tom Darbyshire said that the only way he could get a real runaway out of his mules was to "throw the lines away, By Goll, keep up an Indian whoop, By Goll, and pour the whip into them every step of the way, By Goll."

But of all the happenings, carrying water to the work hands in the field at harvest time gave me the biggest kick of all. With a horned saddle strapped over a smelly sheepskin, a gentle old mare, a gallon jug with a strap fastened to the handle to loop over the saddle horn, stirrups buckled up where I could get my feet into them and a whole day before me — that was my idea of the good life.

I filled the jug at the force pump and corked it with a fresh corncob, sidled the old mare alongside the board fence, hung the jug over the saddle horn and climbed on. Then I turned the old mare toward the harvest field, where half a dozen men were at work.

Pap drove an old Eagle dropper, which chuckled along cutting a four-foot swath and dropping the bundles every two or three rods. The field was divided into four stations, with a man on each station. He was supposed to set in right behind the dropper when it came along and bind the grain into sheaves, using a band made of twisted whisps of straw. Each binder was supposed to cover his section before the dropper came around again. To get "caught" by the reaper before the station was all bound was considered an everlasting dis-grace.

Mounted on my charger, I made the rounds of these harvest hands with my jug of cool water. And they were always ready for me too. They would pull out the stopper, slop out a little water to rinse off the mouth of the jug, and then turn it up and gurgle down a quart or so. When it came to watering Pap, the old mare would generally shy considerable at the dropper, and sometimes it took several tacks before I got her close enough to hand him the jug. Pap never admitted he was thirsty, but he always drank more water than any other man on the job.

Then I would return to the well, fill the jug with fresh water, climb on and head back to the field. There I was, guiding a big, strong horse all by myself, swatting a greenhead that lit on her shoulder or riding through a weed patch eight fcct high. Talk about luxury, or heaven — it was all those with some to spare!

The only other experience that approached this one in boyhood pleasures came when I was old enough to go along to the timber to salt the cattle. The timber was four miles from home, wild and lonely and without any sign of a fence. Our neighbors turned their cattle loose in the woods when pastures got short in mid-summer.

All the animals had to be branded, of course, and our brand was a large "O."

Sometimes it was hard to find our woods cattle, for the timber was thick and stretched for miles. There were always other droves running loose at the same time and they all had some kind of a bellweather. We would ride into the cool woods, ford a creek or two, climb the great hills and finally catch the faint tinkle of a bell far in the distance. But like as not, when we reached the cattle, they were not ours — so off we went in another direction. It was always such fun to ride through the woods that I used to hope we wouldn't find our cattle for a long time.

But finally we always found them. As soon as they caught sight of us they came running and bawling, hungry for the taste of salt. My brother would open the sack, dip out big handfuls and drop them on the ground. The cattle would surge in, pushing and shoving and acting as greedy as hogs. Often they would get a mouthful of salt and slobber so much that it all ran down to the ground. Once I saw a steer take a lump big as a pint cup and chew it down without batting an eye.

Then came the ride home. My brother always chose a way that led away off and around, to give the impression that he was lost. Then he'd say that we might have to spend the night in the woods. It was great fun for a boy, believe me.

I have often wondered what city boys find to do just for fun. All cluttered up with houses and laid out in streets with no horses or mules, or cattle or dogs, or guns — it must be pretty dull.

prairie
storms

I don't know why it was, but when I was a boy on the farm, I was most scared to death of storms. Any sort of a little cloud was a threat, and a big, black one caused me to fairly shake in my boots. Lightning and thunder drove me right down into the cellar if it was in the daytime, and deep under covers, head and ears, if it was in the night. Yet I never was struck by lightning, or killed by a storm, but I must have suffered more from fright than if I had been.

Maybe it was because we lived so much out of doors, and could see what a big thing a summer storm is. Big rippers used to come down from the northwest on summer afternoons about five o'clock. The whole sky out that way would be black as ink, but in it — not so very high up — would be a grayish band of clouds that meant wind a plenty. Every little bit a great red streak of lightning would sizzle down across the black face of the clouds, then thunder would rumble closer and closer, and let you know that you were in for it this time if you didn't watch out.

The wind would still be in the east, though, and I used to hope that it would prove strong enough to hold the storm back. The folks used to say that the storm was coming up against the wind. It seemed to me that it must be a whopper to be able to do that. That was long before we ever heard of stratum currents, and we supposed that all the wind there was always traveled in the same direction.

But pretty soon the east wind would stop blowing, and there would be a dead calm. Out in the west you could see a great grayish mess of something, right down on the ground, and coming to beat the band. A minute later it struck, and that ornery looking nightmare on the ground turned out to be dust, picked up and carried along by the wind. The trees would begin to bend away over, chickens would go scurrying to shelter, hogs would squeal, the cattle would run under the sheds, and the field hands would come swarming in with the work horses, yet like as not get caught before they reached the barn.

When the wind got right down to business a little later, the trees and bushes would bend over pretty near to the ground, and maybe a lot of limbs would break off. Loose boards would go clattering along the ground, there was a frightful roaring sound, and every whip-stitch a blinding flash. Right after it there would be a clap of thunder that would shake the dishes in the cupboard, and just about scare a body to death.

By this time it was so dark that it might as well be night. Then the rain would come dashing down, a blinding sheet of water that shut off all view of everything outside just like a wall. Maybe it would last that way for half an hour and then slack up a little. But just when you began to think the worst might be over, the wind would shift to another quarter and come with a side-swiping blast that was worse than the first one. The trees now bent in a fresh direction and another deluge came down. But the house was still standing, and we were in the dry, and after a while Pap would say the storm was letting up and we took on fresh hope.

Pretty soon the thunder would be rumbling harmlessly away off to the southeast, and only a lot of big lazy raindrops kept coming down. A light streak in the west told us that the storm was broken up, and we were safe again, at least 'til the next one came along. Then just as we were beginning to have some fun wading barefoot in the water, a terrific streak of forked lightning would come whipping back from the storm, right overhead, and there would be a muttering crash of thunder. It would kind of taper off and come back in echoes, and thump and rumble around for quite a spell, and wind up with a boom or two that seemed to shake the whole county.

Then the rainbow would begin to form across the east, getting brighter and brighter as the sun came out more 'til it stood clean across the sky as pretty as anything could be. And right over there in John Tucker's field was the end of it, and a sack of gold. But every time we ever tried to get it, something happened to the rainbow. It either petered out or changed its location before we got there, so we finally quit trying. It was always awfully wet going anyhow.

Everywhere about the place there would be little gullies washed out by the rain, and in the fields, where the ground was soft, some great big ones. All the low ground would be under water, and up would come the creek, just booming with black water. It would be all cluttered up with rails, limbs of trees, grain bundles, every kind of rubbish you ever heard of, and sometimes the wreck of a wooden bridge. Once some drowned chickens came floating down, and a dead hog, and a privy, and a lot of ear corn. It was fun to stand on the bridge and try to spear things as they came under, but we never had much luck at it. We never had any tools to work with except what we could find along the fences, and it's hard to jab a wooden stick into anything and make it hold.

We did manage one time to fasten onto a dead dog that came down in the freshet. Pierkses two boys, one of 'em, got an eye on him first when it was a hundred yards off, coming fast, and riding low in the water. We hurried and got a forked limb and broke the branches off a foot from the fork, and stood there all ready for it. There was a sharp bend just above the bridge, and the current slammed the dog right over against the bank. One of the Flamm boys was posted over there — barefooted, of course — on the slickest kind of a bank, that slanted a right smart toward the water. When the dog brushed along the bank right under him, he couldn't help trying for him. He did get it by the hind leg but the current was too swift and set up quite a pull. We all ran over to help him, but we didn't get there in time, and George slipped right down into that black water.

Before you could blink an eye George was underneath the bridge, his head bumping along against the timbers, for the water came up to within three inches of the bridge. But right away he popped out on the other side, and we all scampered down the north bank to help him out, if he needed help. But he was a good swimmer and pretty soon he got hold of a sour dock root that was sticking out of the bank, and crawled out as slick as you please. He was sure a wet boy, but we were all pretty wet by this time for a drizzling rain had set in more than an hour before. But we didn't mind that when as many things were floating in the creek as there were that day.

By this time the dog was a hundred yards below us and going at a good clip. It looked like we were going to lose him. But we took a long run — maybe a quarter of a mile ahead of him — and at a place where a line fence was washed out, got a pole and stretched it across kind of slantwise. When the dog came down a minute later he hit the pole, and the current slid him over to our side and we nabbed him and dragged him out. He was a genuine Newfoundland, most as big as a calf.

But we soon found out that he hadn't been drowned in that flood. He had a bullet hole in his forehead, one of his ears was gone, and on several places on his body the hair had slipped off. So we calculated that he had been dead several days, and the freshet had picked him up and was floating him off. We hated to see a fine dog like that dead. But there was no helping it now. We couldn't think of any use we could make of him so we rolled him back into the water and let him go.

Just then we heard Pap calling us. When we got up by the barn where he was, he told us that the storm had blown down about forty rods of rail fence, and that the cattle were in the young corn. Then all hands went running down there to drive the cattle out and lay up that fence.

Pap certainly knew all about building a rail fence. He had a home-made tool — with a crossbar on it — that he set down in line with two or three stakes where the fence ought to be, to show how much worm to use. He would lay the lower rail and lap, and it was our job to lay up all the rest. We had to have the corners straight up and down and fasten them with lock-rails to hold them there. It isn't so very hard to do when the rails are dry. But take a mess of wet rails, sometimes half buried under mud that had washed off the fields, and it was the most particular kind of a job to get a rail fence to stand up straight 'til you got the lockers on.

Next morning Pap found out that the lower flood gate was washed out by the freshet, and that the stock was liable to get into Schomp's field. That would never do. It would make Schomp mad for one thing, and worse than that, his fields were all alive with cockle-burs. The cattle would get them on their tails and scatter them all over our place and cause no end of trouble getting rid of them.

So right after breakfast we hitched up a team to the big wagon, loaded in tools, wire, planks, and every-thing, and drove through the soft fields to the lower line fence to fix the flood gate.

By this time the water had run down 'til it wasn't over two feet deep in the creek, but the banks were all smeared over with mud, where the high water had been — and the slickest, slimiest mud you ever saw. But no matter about that, the flood gate had to be fixed right away, so we rolled our britches high as we could and went right at it.

It wasn't such a bad job, especially for a youngster,

and we liked it better than common work. We dug two holes for the anchor posts, and got about as muddy as pigs doing it. Then we slid a log across and tied it to the anchors. We strung a set of wires down from this log and fastened planks and poles to them to make the gate, and at the bottom put a heavy pole to hold everything down straight. All this was fixed so that when a flood came along the gate would lift with the rising water, and close down again as the water got lower. It was a good theory but hardly ever worked. Generally drift wood got clogged and choked in the flood gate and made the water back up, sometimes a quarter of a mile, 'til finally the weight got to where the whole thing gave way and floated off down the creek.

Bad as storms were in the daytime, though, they were a good many times worse at night. In daylight you can see *how* you are getting killed, but at night you haven't the slightest show at all. A fellow's feelings, when a night storm is coming up, are about as uncomfortable as anything could possibly be.

I always slept in a corner room upstairs with my brother Frank. There were two windows on the west and one on the north. Nobody could possibly have set them better to let in all the lightning and thunder. No matter how hot the night was, I burrowed deep down under the covers — close up to Frank as I could squeeze — and sweat, and sizzled, and suffocated with my fingers in my ears all through every storm that came up. Once in a while I would peep out to see if it had quit, but like as not a thunderbolt big as a stovepipe would let loose right in my face and back I would duck for another half hour.

That big brother I slept with was mighty little help, for he could sleep like a baby right through the worst kind of storms. He didn't appear to have any sense about danger at all. Finally, after I was pretty near drowned in sweat, the storm would let up, and I never forgot to thank God for that. Nothing can be sweeter than to hear the thunder rumbling away off in the southeast, and see the stars shining once more. My goodness, what a relief it was!

drouth,
windmills
and
tramps

As a general thing it rained every few days during
the spring and early part of summer, and then slowed
up a good deal and only rained once in a while for a
month or two. But two or three different years there
wasn't very much rain at all and things got pretty dry.
The tires began to come off the wagon wheels, and
hoops to loosen on tubs and such things. The water in

the creek dried up and the wells got so low that every time we watered the cows we pumped the wells dry. Then the cows that hadn't had a drink yet would stand around and fight flies and wait, and maybe in an hour or so enough water would seep in so we could finish up the job.

One year when it hardly rained at all after summer set in, all the wells in the neighborhood went dry. Fortunately on the Mussack farm there was a well that they said had a big spring in it, and couldn't be pumped dry. So a lot of different people drove their cattle over there to get water. It wasn't such a very hard job to work the handle and just make the water boil up, either. The water stood up to within two or three feet of the top, it didn't have to be lifted very far, and that's what made it pump so easy.

I have seen as many as five or six droves of stock cattle and cows herded down around Mussack's farm, taking turns at getting watered. Some people drove their stock as much as four or five miles to water there. But since it was pretty hot, by the time they walked back home again those cattle would be about as thirsty as ever. Then they would mill around and bellow and bawl like everything.

So everybody got busy trying to locate water on his own farm. In those days all the wells were dug by hand, and mostly were eighteen to twenty feet deep. A lot of people didn't even have a pump, but rigged up a contrivance over the well called a sweep. It was made of two parts, one a post with a forked top that stood maybe fifteen or sixteen feet high, off to one side of the well several steps. Across this post and fastened by a bolt somewhere near the middle — in the crotch — was a great long pole, the butt end resting on the ground and the small end hoisted away up in the air. From this small end a rope dangled down and on the end of it was a bucket. You could pull down on the rope and lower the bucket into the water and then pull the rope to hoist her up. A rock or some other weight would be fastened on the butt end of the sweep to balance the bucket of water, so it didn't take much of a pull to bring it up.

The well stood open at the top, but a kind of box was built around it called a curb. Kids seldom fell in, but once in a while a chicken would lose its balance and go down the well, and I remember when three white geese got in some way. But Pap let one of the boys down on the rope, to tie a goose at a time to the bucket, so it wasn't long 'til they all were out. The boy stayed down at the surface of the water until the last goose was out. That wasn't hard to do though, because the well was lined with rocks, and these stuck out into the well so you could stick your toe in and even climb up and down.

The geese didn't seem to worry very much about being down there for they are natural born swimmers and can sit on the water all day — and I suppose all night, as far as that goes. But I never saw a chicken or a turkey taken out of the well alive. Maybe if we had discovered them soon after they fell in, it would have been different. But they can't stay up long in water, and pretty soon down they go. It's several days before they get light enough to float, and that's the first you know they are in there. Generally, if the men were not too busy in the fields, they pumped the well dry after fishing out anything that was dead and in most cases it filled up with water again in a few hours. But whether it was pumped out or not, I never heard of any harm coming of it.

One extra dry year, when the wells were all failing and we had to pump for the cattle out of three or four different ones, Pap took a notion to try for water in the old lake bed on our south forty. For one thing it was the lowest ground on the farm, so he figured that he might not have to dig so far to reach water.

We hitched a team up to the big wagon, loaded in spades and shovels and a jug of drinking water, and of course I went along, boy like. We set up at the lower edge of the lake bed about a rod from where the division fence ran across. Pap and one of the boys went right to digging and by dinner time had struck quicksand with water in it, not a bit over four feet down. When we got back after dinner, there was six inches of water in the bottom of that shallow hole.

It was in the fall of the year and the blackbirds were gathering up to go south. A great swarm of them came by, fairly darkening the sun, and lit along the bank of the creek, likely as not looking for water. The field along that creek bank was just covered with blackbirds, several rods back from the bank, for a quarter of a mile, and such a jabbering you never heard.

The boys slid down and dipped the water out, best they could, and went to digging again. Joe ran his spade down into the bottom of that hole and struck something. He thought at first that it might be a chunk of wood or something. But when he pried it up, it was a great big mud turtle — the size of a washpan. He got it by the tail and hoisted it out, and didn't seem to think so very much about it, but all at once he ran his spade against another turtle, as big and ugly and smelly as the first one. Inside of an hour the boys dug up and threw out of that well eleven big mud turtles.

They didn't seem to have much life in them, and laid still where the men tossed them. Even when you put a lighted match to the end of their tails they didn't cut many capers. We didn't know what to make of it but Chauncey Blodgett happened along that afternoon, and told us that these turtles "hibergated," or something like that. He said they burrowed down below the frost line and lived that way until about the time the first thunder and lightning came.

That was the funniest well you ever saw. The men couldn't get it dug any deeper than about four feet, no matter how hard or fast they dug. The water just came surging in on all sides and from the bottom, and the edges crumbled off and caved in as fast as they scooped out the quicksand. Pap was determined to dig deeper, but it wasn't any use to try. By the middle of the afternoon that well was eight or nine feet across at the bottom and only four feet deep. They had heaved out tons of quicksand in the last three hours without deepening the well an inch.

So we drove the team to the house and Pap got the saw and hammer, and we picked up a lot of stray fence planks, and some two by fours, and went back and made a square curb for that wild well. When they got it ready they upended it and dropped it into the hole. It was boarded up about five feet, and the corner posts stuck up six or seven feet in the air. The idea was to nail more boards on as the well was deepened and the curb sunk down.

The men got to digging again, and Pap and I stood on the edges of the curb to force it down. Little by little we could feel it settle. It was a good scheme all right, for that curb held back the sand from caving in, and it was easy to heave out just what was inside it. In that way we finally got the well to a depth of about seven feet, but there the curb stuck, solid as a church, and all of us together couldn't budge it an inch. The quicksand had settled all around it and wedged it fast, so we had to quit trying to deepen the well and let it go at that. The last hour or so we hadn't done much good at it anyway, for the water came in so fast it took about all the men's time baling it out.

In ten minutes after the digging stopped, there was three feet of water in that well. The men pulled a big wooden pump out of a dry well and put it in, and nobody could pump fast enough to lower that water six inches. It was a good enough well to have watered all the cattle in the county, I reckon. That old lake bed, twenty acres or more, was just naturally underlaid with quicksand and filled with water. You might as well try to pump a river dry.

As soon as they had the trough set up and leveled off, Pap sent two of the boys to drive the cattle down for a drink. The way they did swig down that fresh water was a sight. I don't pretend to say how much water an old cow can drink when she is good and thirsty, but to put it mildly, I should say a barrel, anyway. They don't drink fast but they stay at it a long time.

Generally they moisten up their insides with two or three gallons, then stop and breathe, think it over a little, and really enjoy it. Then they will start in again. Pretty soon you can see a hollow place in their flanks begin to fill out. Like as not they will take another rest, and swing their heads around over their shoulder to scare off the flies. Then they will set in to drink in dead earnest, and swig, and swig, until their sides swell away out and you think they surely will burst. When they finally waddle away from the trough they look just like a blown-up balloon.

It takes rivers of water to satisfy a bunch of thirsty cows. I have pumped, and pumped, and pumped, until I lost all sense of what I was doing. Over at the Mussack farm one of the Peckham boys, on a hot evening, pumped himself sick. They had to bathe his temples with vinegar, rub salt on the back of his neck, and put a horse radish poultice on the bottoms of his feet, to bring him to.

That same fall Pap bought a brand new Eureka windmill and set it up over our new well, and I reckon that was the cleverest thing he ever did. First we used to go down there and throw her in gear and watch the cattle drink for an hour or two, 'til they were all satisfied, and then throw her out of gear again. But after a while it got to be more common to us and we used to just leave her in gear all the time. There was no end of water, to begin with, nor wind either, for that matter. So we kept it well greased and just let her flicker, day and night, whenever the wind was blowing.

Next year Pap built a big round tank, that held as many as fifteen or twenty barrels of water. I captured a good sized catfish out of the creek once and put him into that tank, and he lived all summer there and seemed to like it all right. In the fall I put him back into the creek, because the winters got awful cold and that tank would surely freeze solid to the bottom if we left any water in it.

The windmill had a big long tail which held the wheel facing the wind. To throw it out of gear you pulled down on a long lever, and a wire that ran up to the top works pulled on another lever, and lifted a big iron ball that was there to hold things in working position. Then the tail would whip around alongside the wheel and the wind would catch it and swing the whole thing around so that the edge of the wheel pointed into the wind and she stopped whirling right there.

One Saturday afternoon I had been prowling around the willow thicket down that way, hunting a few york-nuts and Indian arrow heads, and went over to the windmill to get a drink. Then I climbed up the ladder to the little platform about three feet across, at the top of the tower, to study the mechanism of the wonderful machine that pumped all our stock water. I saw this big iron ball fastened by a set screw to a lifting rod. It was set about two thirds of the way down. Why, I began to wonder, was it set just exactly where it was. Wouldn't it work just as well in some other position? If it was out more toward the end of the rod, wouldn't it work faster?

Bulging over with curiosity, I ran to the barn — a quarter of a mile away — for a monkey wrench, hurried back, scaled that tower again, and with the monkey wrench loosened the set screw that held the big iron weight fast. Then I slid it up several inches nearer the end of the rod, and climbed down to try it out. I unhooked the gear lever and tested out the pull to see whether it was more than before. I could notice quite a difference. I let the gear lever lift an inch at a time, in order to get all the fun out of it there was to be had. Just then I heard an awful thump, a board in the well platform was shivered across one end, and the big iron weight went rolling down the bank. I had neglected to fasten down the miserable set screw, and that forty pound weight had slipped off the end and fallen not more than six inches from my head.

I was terribly scared. I felt my legs shaking, and sat down on the platform and broke out in a cold sweat. Then I poured out my feelings on that confounded set screw. I don't think I ever blamed myself for tinkering with the thing. Kids are not built that way, and a lot of grown up people are a good deal the same way.

When my wits finally came back I fished that big weight out of the creek and did my level best to carry it up the ladder to put it back in place. But I couldn't cut the mustard. It was about all I could do to lift it, say nothing about climbing a ladder with it. I did get up three or four feet from the ground a time or two, but soon found out that it was no use.

That evening, after supper, I told Frank that the weight had fallen off the wind pump, and he was for going down to fix it right away. I motioned to him to keep still about it, and we slinked out without being noticed. Frank said we would have to take the monkey wrench along and went to the currycomb box to get it, but it was not there. We hunted high and low but couldn't find it. So we took another kind of wrench out of the self binder box and went down. Frank wasn't sure that the wrench would fit, but I never once let on that I knew anything about the monkey wrench. You can't expect a boy to put tools back after using them.

When we got near the windmill I made some excuse to run on ahead, intending to pick up the monkey wrench and pretend that I had brought it from the barn. But it was nowhere to be seen. Frank noticed that I was scouting for something and asked me what I had lost. I told him, "Oh, only a yorknut," and that seemed to satisfy him. Then, without any more fuss, he climbed up the ladder with that big weight under his arm, just as slick as a whistle. I followed right below him and we both crawled out onto the little platform up there.

There was the monkey wrench, right on that platform! How it ever got there was a seven days' wonder. I knew nothing about it, of course, and Frank couldn't make it out. He told the folks about it and they all puzzled over it for quite a while.

It remained a complete mystery. Nobody could figure it out, and as far as I know, this is the first time the truth has been told about that monkey wrench. It bothered me quite a bit at first to keep it to myself, when it was such a big mystery to everybody. Then my interest in it began to taper off and years ago I thought I had outlived it. But I really feel a little bit relieved, even at this late day, that I have come right out with it at last.

An awful lot of tramps were around that dry summer. I can remember how those ragged, dirty men would come strolling up the road and ask for something to eat and maybe for a chance to work. Mother always fixed something for everyone that came along. I have seen her stop her other work and fry eggs, and ham, and potatoes for them, and set out three or four thick slices of bread, and a hunk of butter, and make them coffee, and fuss around like they were some kin to her. She had such a big heart that she never could stand it to see anybody want for anything, especially if it was in her power to give it to them.

We had more tramps call at our house than anybody else, I believe. Andy Cline, who kept a store at Yarmouth where the folks used to do their trading, told Mother that the tramps had a way of marking places where the women folks would feed them well, and that the more of them she fed, the more of them would come. But that kind of talk didn't seem to have any effect on Mother. She always claimed that what little she gave that way didn't amount to anything much, and she would rather feed a hundred scamps than refuse one honest man who was hungry. Anyhow she kept right on feeding them, and two or three different times one of them insisted on doing work about the place to pay for it.

One hot day in June a good looking fellow about thirty years old knocked at the kitchen door and asked Mother if he could pull some weeds out of the sweet corn patch to earn his breakfast. It was then ten o'clock in the forenoon, and that poor fellow hadn't had a bite to eat that day. Mother told him to go ahead, and soon as she could get something ready she would call him. But he told her not to bother about getting anything special for him, just to wait until noon, and he would eat when the rest did. So he went to work pulling weeds, and worked just like the garden belonged to him.

About half past eleven Mother took him out a big dipperful of cold buttermilk she kept hanging down the well, and the way the fellow guzzled that down was a sight. He never stopped to draw breath or anything 'til that dipper of buttermilk was all down. Then he thanked her, and bowed away down low, and went on pulling weeds, right up to the time the men came in to wash up for dinner. He stood around and waited 'til everybody else was through, then got a big washpanful of water from the cistern pump and soaped and scrubbed himself like he enjoyed it. He wouldn't come to the table with the rest of us, but insisted on eating off of a box out under the silver ash trees, all by himself. I kept one eye on him all the time. He put away as much food as I ever saw anybody do — and we had some big eaters in the neighborhood, too.

After dinner the men went out to sit around in the

breeze in the shade until the horses were done eating, but that tramp took down a scythe that was hanging in a plum tree and went to cutting weeds in the back yard. He kept right at it after the men went to work in the fields, and never stopped 'til he had mowed the whole yard and had it looking like yards did in the towns.

By that time Mother was out in the garden picking gooseberries. The tramp came out and went at it also, and picked more than four quarts. Then he picked about three gallons of cherries, and went out to the wood pile to chop and split wood the rest of the afternoon. Anybody who ever chopped wood knows that summer is no time to do it. It is one of the hottest jobs that ever was, in summer, and mighty few can stand to do it.

That evening, when the men were sitting around in the cool, Pap asked the fellow what his name was. He replied that it was Nebuchadnezzar, that he used to be a king of the Jews, and that this was his second time on earth. He said that the man he worked for in Burlington had run off with another man's wife, that same night his mill burned down, and a few days later the woman he was eloping with had robbed him of every cent he had in the world, and run away with still another man. This was too much for the employer, so he went down to the banks of the Mississippi about midnight and jumped off of a barge, at the deepest place he could find, and hadn't been seen or heard of since.

With the business for which he was trained shot all to smithereens, Nebuchadnezzar had struck out afoot and had walked all over Minnesota, Nebraska, and parts of Missouri trying to find work. Finally he had straggled into our front yard because he had seen a tramps mark on the gate post and knew he could get a bite to eat.

It all sounded reasonable enough except that Nebuchadnezzar stuff. None of us could figure out what the fellow meant by that kind of talk. He slept in the barn that night and went to the fields with the men next day, hunted cockleburs and Canada thistles all through the young corn, straightened up ten rods of worm fence, trimmed the hedge fence around the apple orchard, and killed a big black snake. When he came in with the men for dinner, he took Mother around the waist and gave her the biggest kind of a hug, in spite of all the squirming and dodging she could do. She scolded him about such rough actions and told him she would be afraid to tell Annison about it for fear he would shoot him on the spot.

Nebuchadnezzar couldn't hold out any longer so up and told us that he was Mort Cox, a full cousin of Mother's from Cooperstown, Illinois. He had come over for a little visit with us, to see the beautiful new country where we lived. I never saw anybody so taken back and as tickled as Mother was. She was awfully relieved, and ran to tell Pap.

He came in and shook Mort good, and they began to talk about all the folks back in Brown county — the Henry's, the Legg's, the Orchard's, the McKinnon's and a dozen or so other families they used to know when they lived on a stump farm away back on Crooked creek, before they traded farms with a lonesome old bachelor and came to the prairies of Iowa.

We saw some tramps every summer. They seeemed to be going nowhere in particular, were always dirty, ragged, and hungry, and mighty few of them ever stuck to it very long if you gave them a job at good wages. But when times got a little better the tramps gradually thinned out. Some folks said they took to the railroads and lived off the town people. Maybe that was it. I don't know. All I know is that they were a shiftless lot as a general thing, and didn't take to work or water. But I never heard of any of them getting into any trouble with the law. I reckon they were too good-for-nothing and didn't have get-up enough even to steal.

thrashing

time

It generally takes a long time to build a fortune, but it only takes a few weeks or months to grow a crop. There is nothing more interesting than to watch the plants get higher and stronger, day by day, until they fully mature and reproduce their kind. And it is interesting to figure on how much life can be wrapped up in a small seed of grain.

Pap went to the centennial at Philadelphia, and brought home a ten cent tobacco sack of Russian oats, from which we finally got seed enough to sow forty acres. They were the whoppingest oats anybody ever saw, and actually grew to be as high as Pap himself — and he was a six footer. One thing about this oat was that a single seed would produce sometimes a dozen or more stems. "Stooling out" was what the folks called it. I heard Pap say that he found one where he counted forty-seven stalks that had all formed from one oat seed.

Next year all the neighbors just had to have some of those wonderful Russian oats. So they traded with Pap, and secured enough to sow their entire acreage. It all did mighty well, too, and grew to be most six feet high. But just before it was ready to be cut, a terrible storm came along and dashed it flat to the ground. You never saw such a mess in your life. Twisted and tangled in every shape, it was a problem what to do with it. Some folks just cut it with mowers and stacked it up for cow feed. But Pap was bound to harvest his if there was any way to do it.

He started in with the new Minneapolis twine binder. But if you cut the way the heads mostly lay, the harvester would just push the grain down and slide right over it. Going against the way it leaned, the sickle guards just buried themselves under a great mass of tangled grain, and the elevators got clogged right up. So Pap decided to cut the field all one way, and cut only half a swath at a time so the elevators could handle it.

It was my job to walk behind the binder and rake

the grain down into the beaters that made the bundle. It was a steady job, believe me. If I missed one stroke the whole thing would clog up, and the bull wheel would begin to drag. Then Pap would climb down off his high perch on the driving seat, claw out the clogged grain and free the mechanism so that it was possible to go ahead. Once across the field he would turn the machine around and drive back to the starting point light, which means without cutting at all. On this return trip I was allowed to jump onto the rear frame, behind the reel, and ride if I could hold on. Then came another turn through the tangled grain, and back and forth and back and forth until we had that terrible crop finally bound up into bundles, such as they were.

We had to cut the grain very low down, and with oats five or six feet long the bundles were of enormous size. Sometimes three or four of them would be so tangled together that the shockers just tumbled them into the orneriest kind of shocks and let it go at that. I never saw such a shock field. The ground was half covered with them. When we came to thrash that crop there was hardly room in the field to stack the straw.

That cooked the Russian oats in our neighborhood for good and all, and we went back to the good old brands that had proved fit for Iowa soil and climate. Oats two or three feet tall do not blow down like a crop that has stretched up six feet.

Of all the work we were called upon to do in course of the year, there was nothing that quite compared in genuine classic flavor with thrashing. Our neighbors —

maybe fifteen of us — would all thrash together, helping one another in turn until we all were through.
That meant going to a new place every day or two and
eating the best food the women could cook.

Each woman seemed to try to outdo all the rest in
the variety and quality of her cooking. We got so much
fried chicken day after day that we honestly got tired of
it. Some of the folks would have fresh beef and that
was a mighty good treat, because we hardly ever got any
beef. Once in a long time a beef wagon would drive
through the country from Mediapolis, or New London,
but there were not enough customers to make it pay
and they didn't try it very often.

Pap always killed a mutton for thrashers and I
thought there was nothing better than fresh mutton
when you were about starved. That was the condition
we were always in when the woman of the house came
out and banged on a dishpan with a potato masher —
the signal to come and wash up for dinner.

It was a sight to see — twenty farm hands washing
up for dinner. Most houses had only one washpan for
regular use, but on these occasions something else
would serve the purpose and maybe as many as three
could wash at a time. First the man pumped water out
of a cistern and placed the washpans on the platform
or bench, then dipping up a double handful, soaped
up for a good scrubbing. Some of the men had the habit
of blowing their hands while they were washing their
faces. It made a funny sound — just made the soapsuds
boil. With rolled up sleeves they would wash as far as

the elbows, and dry themselves all on the same towel. When one got too wet another one would be started. But that generally exhausted the supply, and the last four or five men would have to wring out the towels to get any good of them. Then those that had hair would all comb up, and look pretty respectable.

Generally the women would fix it so that all could eat at once, but sometimes they didn't have enough dishes to do that so the men had to eat in relays. A fellow who was already hungry as a bear sometimes had to sit back and watch another lot eat. Then when he did get his inning, a good many things that ought to be hot were cold and not so good. That was the reason there was always a scramble for the first table. You couldn't blame the men either.

But la, me there was an abundance for all and a lot to spare besides. There was every kind of thing that grows on a farm — potatoes, cabbage, beets, onions, apple sauce, and always the mighty good kind of meat. Home-made bread and pies, several kinds of jam, spiced relishes, pickles, green beans, corn on the cob you spread all over with butter and ate right out of your hands — all was on deck. There was pie, cake, coffee, tea, milk, doughnuts and everything you ever heard of. Sometimes there were things you had never heard of — and you ate them on faith.

One of the things I remember about those old times was the great numbers of flies that infested every farm home. It seems strange that people lived on earth thousands of years before anybody ever thought of screens to keep the flies out of houses. I was nearly a man grown before door and window screens were introduced.

Before that it was a battle from June to November, when the frost got the flies for good. How the women ever managed to do any cooking without getting flies mixed into it is more than I can understand. There were literally millions of them swarmed in the kitchens, attracted by the odor of cooking.

Just before dinner was called there was an order to drive flies. Half a dozen women would arm themselves with dishcloths, towels, papers and tree twigs, and shake them with great vigor all about the room. The flies would move out the door like a swarm of bees, but the effort never came anywhere near getting all of them. Even so, those they succeeded in driving out were mostly all back within a minute or so.

While we were seated at table three or four women would do nothing else but drive back flies. Armed with fly brushes — which were generally made up of strips of paper fastened on a rod — they would get after every fly that ventured upon the table. If they missed a stroke or two, maybe to pass something, here the flies would come and settle down on everything. It was ticklish business, for if you happened to swallow one of those flies with your food it made you mighty sick, as any farm hand can tell you.

Once when we were eating thrashing dinner, at the Manson farm, Old Mrs. Manson came in with milk for the coffee, saying as she did so: "Here's fresh milk, men, fer your coffee. 'Tain't even been strained. Well, I did sorter strain it through my apern when I was milkin' the cow, but that's all."

Nobody at the table seemed to appreciate the extra value Mrs. Manson placed on her milk because of its not having been strained, but she must have been pretty proud of it, for she went over it several times before dinner was through.

During the meal, a fly dropped into a cup of coffee at Dave Michaels' place, and Dave passed it up to Mrs. Manson expecting a fresh cupful. But she dipped the fly out with the corner of her apron and handed the cup right back to him, remarking: "Some men is mighty hepless." Poor Dave went without coffee that meal.

There were all kinds of cooks and all kinds of places to eat, and all kinds of things to eat. Generally they were about as good as any human being ever tasted.

After dinner the thrashing hands sat around in the shade while the boys struck up all kinds of athletic sports. But we never called them athletic in those days — in fact we had never heard of athletics.

Chinning was a common favorite. It was done by grasping a pole with both hands and drawing your body up until you could stick your chin over the pole, then letting down to arms length and pulling up again. The one who could do that the greatest number of times was the champion. Moritz Fisher chinned himself twenty times once. A good many could do it as many as fifteen times.

The first five or six hoists are easy enough but then it

begins to grow tiresome. By the time a dozen is passed it is real hard, and the last four or five lifts are just the hardest kind of work. It required more effort to do a turn chinning than to perform a day's ordinary work, but there is no kind of a game in just plain work. There *was* in chinning, and that was no doubt its charm.

Rolling the barrel was good too. We would take an empty barrel and go over it heels first, lying flat on our backs and inching over by hand power. It looks easy enough but there comes a time — just as you think you are going to make it — when the balance goes against you and unless you are lucky, you are liable to land on your head. I have seen a good many pretty smart fellows fairly scalp themselves when they came heaving back on their heads at the turning point of that game.

Lifting the wagon tongue was another good game. A fellow lay down under the tongue with his feet toward the wagon. Then he was supposed to grasp the tongue with both hands and get up with it. The trick was to maneuver the thing so as not to move the wagon forward. And, of course, you were not allowed to lock the wagon. Anybody could do it with the wagon locked.

Square Holts was another wonderful game. Two men would sit on the ground facing each other with their feet against a board. Then they would grasp a fork handle and see which could pull the other up. It took a good grip to do that and you had to know how to keep your weight near the ground. The fellows who sat up straight to pull were never in it at all. We had some mighty good square holt pullers in our crowd and there were not many who dared challenge them. When they did, they got yanked up mighty quick, believe me.

And jump: we used to do every kind of jumping act that was ever heard of, and we had some real experts at it too. Barnett Hale was a man of some fifty years and stood kind of stooping-forward like, with a short body and awfully long legs. He was a carpenter by trade as well as a farmer, and had built nearly all the barns and houses in the country. He liked to tell that when he was a young man he used to be able to do a running hop-skip-and-jump of forty-five feet, and of course we believed him. It was the ambition of the best of our crowd to at least equal Barnett Hale's record.

I do not know how many weeks time I put in trying that myself. Plowing corn in the field barefoot, I used to use all the time that the horses were resting at practicing to hop-skip-and-jump. I calculated the distance by the corn rows. Week by week I could see that I was gaining a little. Noontime, while waiting for the horses to finish their hay, I put in the entire time hopping, skipping, and jumping. The pep that is stored up in youth for this sort of thing is beyond belief. We were never tired of any kind of sport or game. But I never quite reached the record of Barnett Hale. Forty-two feet was my absolute limit, but I could beat anybody in our crowd as far as that is concerned, or anybody else I ran across.

We had broad jumpers who could leap twelve feet with the use of weights, and that was the way we did it. We had high jumpers, and high kickers, and two or three of the boys were good at foot racing. Charlie Plunkett, son of the village doctor, was the leader of the bunch. He could do a hundred yards at about ten and a half seconds. John Fye was about as good and Elt Conklin was not a bit slow. But Elt was a religious boy and never mixed with us in the sports to any great extent.

But the prime sport of all was wrestling. We had three or four prize wrestlers who would spend the noon period at thrashing time with one another and all comers. Once in a while some has-been would take a chance, announcing that he could throw anybody in the crowd. Generally he wound up getting a sprained hand or ankle, or something else. You just can't wrestle to amount to anything after you get settled and stiff.

I had a pretty good reputation as a wrestler myself, and wasn't afraid of the best of them. But one time a hired hand of Chauncey Blodgett, a fellow by the name of Kelly, tackled me for a bout. He was short and stubby, and his hair was just like the bristles on a pig. We cavorted around over the barn lot for several minutes, both at our utmost capacity, and finally edged over on a kind of mound made by the remains of a corncob pile of the winter before. We came down on our knees together with great force and lit on a cob that busted my knee cap loose. I almost fainted with pain and was laid up for three or four weeks. And I carry a lame knee with me to this day, as a result of my ambition to beat them all at wrestling.

The older men took a great delight in our antics, urging us on to our utmost endeavor. It's a wonder we were not all crippled for life — and some of us were. But we never quite came up to the records of the older men. Nearly every one of them had done something in the sport or game line — when he was young — that was away beyond anything we could ever do. Maybe they were stretching a point but we believed them then and nearly busted ourselves trying to equal them.

Henry Fye was the boss thrasher of our time. He owned a ten horse rig, which meant that it took ten horses to work the horse power machine. A long tumbling rod connected this with the separator. Then there was a great big cog wheel that engaged the cylinder — the noisiest thing about the machine. It was geared to revolve the toothed cylinder and thrash the grain out of the bundles fed into it by hand by members of the thrashing crew.

The band cutter stood by the side of the feeder, knife in hand, and cut the bands around the bundles so they could be fed into the machine loose. But once in a while a bundle would slip through with the band on, and such a chug you never heard. It would nearly stop the horses on the sweep.

Four or five men worked on the straw pile, the dustiest and dirtiest job you ever saw, and five or six wagons brought the grain in from the field. It was a steady job to measure the grain at the spout with a half bushel measure, and dump it into a wagon box to be hauled away to the bin. It kept a fellow right at it as long as the machine was running, but every once in a while a belt would come off or something would give way. That gave everybody a rest — except the crew, and they had to fix the trouble while we all idled.

It was a great treat to see Henry Fye come driving in to do our thrashing. First the great separator would lumber past — drawn by four big horses and driven by one of the Fye boys, perched away up there ever so high and looking down disdainfully on us poor creatures who never had a chance to go with a thrashing rig. Then would come the horse power and the wagon load of traps and fixings that had to be put together before thrashing could begin. There was a lot of work to it, driving long stakes into the ground to anchor the horse power, leveling and bracing the separator, attaching the carriers, and setting the concaves, screens, and the like. We generally had the thrashing crew overnight, and that furnished a welcome change from having just the family around.

We had about three weeks of this sort of thing every fall, and it was worth all the rest of the plowing, planting and cultivating, to get to go through that experience. Every boy in the neighborhood wanted to grow up to be a thrashing man. But very few of them did. By the time they got to be old enough to do it the charm had worn off. It's the same way with a lot of things.

country cured

Life in the country brought something new every day. Of course there were always some jobs — like plowing corn — that took considerable time. But for the most part, every time one job was finished another and quite different one had to be done. There was spring work, summer work, fall work and still different types of work during the winter season.

Getting up the year's supply of wood started in the fall and continued until late in the winter. It took a right smart of wood to run our place, for we did all the cooking with wood and heated the big house with it. But getting up wood took us to the big timber — a trip we always welcomed.

The old wood heater in the living room took sticks almost four feet long, two armloads at a gulp. But it certainly made things comfortable on a cold day. Our house had eleven rooms, but we tried to heat only three, besides the kitchen. The whole upstairs was always cold as a barn and never had any arrangements for warming. It was supposed to be better for us to sleep in cold rooms anyhow, but it was also a little rough.

During the coldest weather we used to undress and put on our gowns by the heating stove. Then we made a break for bed, through a long hall, up sixteen stair steps, along another hall and across a long bedroom — and without a rag of a carpet the whole way. We jumped into bed shivering like we had a chill, and snuggled under the wool blankets, head and ears, as long as we could hold our breath. After that it was all right until Pap called us next morning.

But it is some chore to roust out of bed in a cold room, when the weather is around zero, and run through the frosty air, bare legged, to the living room to dress. And when we got there, sometimes, the fire was so low that there wasn't a spark of warmth about it. But down under the ashes there was always a bed of live coals, and dry kindling on them soon brought on a roaring fire.

We never measured wood by the cord in those days, but mostly by the load. It took at least forty loads of wood to run our place a year. And it was a big lark to get up that forty loads of wood. We started out with the wagons and wound up with bobsleds when the snow got deep enough and it wasn't storming too bad.

We went a long way for our wood — five or six miles, I should say. We went past the Jim Linder hill, and about a mile below that the fences petered out and then we just followed a sort of trail that wound around away deep into the big woods. Pap owned a ten acre patch of the biggest kind of timber, and to find it was a regular Chinese puzzle. Of course the older boys and Pap knew well enough, but to a youngster it was a mystery how they ever got there and back.

Pap was a wonderful woodsman and handled an axe the best of anybody I ever saw except Charlie Jones. He chopped either right or left handed, and bragged that he never moved out of his tracks to cut down a tree. He left a stump about as square across the top as if you had sawed down the tree, with hardly an axe mark on it.

I always liked to watch Pap logging off. He could stand right on top of a log and whack it into lengths before he ever climbed down, and never bat an eye. I never saw him do it, but he claimed he could cut, split, and rick up seven cords a day. And I wouldn't be surprised if he could do it.

The boys loaded the big timbers first, tied ropes across the standards and over about two thirds of the load, and finished off with poles and limbs 'til the load

was seven or eight feet high. Then we climbed on top
and started the wonderful trip home. There used to be
lots of red sumac berries along the way, and they were
pretty good, too. Then we used to pick red haws, and
black haws, and hazel nuts, and once in a while we
would run onto a wild plum tree, just loaded down with
the finest tasting plums you ever saw. And you could eat
a hundred and they wouldn't hurt you, if you spit out
the seeds.

I used to dig into mice nests around hazel thickets
in the fall and sometimes would find most a quart of
nuts, all shelled out, that the mice had put away for
winter. Some folks robbed the mice of their nuts, but
Pap and Mother never allowed us to. They said the
mice would starve if we took their nuts, and how would
we like it to have our food stolen from us?

The men kept at wood cutting until they had a
woodpile most as big as the barn. Then they commenced to work it up into stove sizes, all split up fine for
the cook stove, with the knotty and gnarly parts sorted
out for the heater. We had a cross-cut saw, a buck saw,
and several axes, and all hands together could make the
work go fast. When we got done there would be the
prettiest pile of nice clean white wood you ever saw,
and chips enough to kindle fires with for a year.

One of my jobs was to clean the ashes out of the
two stoves, and pour them into a great big hopper. By
spring there would be more than twenty-five bushels
piled up there, then Mother would pour water in the
hopper and drain off whole barrels of lye, and a little

later boil it down for soap. She made good soap, too, and always seasoned it with hog grease and bacon rinds and the like. It wasn't like store soap much, just a kind of thick jelly. But it brought out the dirt to beat anything you ever saw.

Mother always kept the soft soap in a barrel, covered up good to keep out the dust, and always kept the barrel out of doors. There wasn't room for it in the kitchen, and she was afraid it would make the meat taste if she kept it in the smokehouse.

We did all our own butchering, of course. Generally butchering time came along in January, in the coldest kind of weather. It took about eleven or twelve big hogs to keep our family in pork for a year, and we generally killed a calf at corn picking time, with a mutton for harvest and thrashing time.

Generally Pap would have a couple or three neighbors come to help us do the butchering. We had a big iron kettle that held thirty gallons and Cappes had a copper one that held even more than that. They hung both of these over a stout pole held up by a couple of chunks of wood, filled them up with water, and built fires under them. A big barrel would be set, slantways like, against the running gears of a bobsled, and that was what they scalded the hogs in, so the hair would slip off.

Pap always used Old Dalsey to shoot the hogs with and generally butchered six at a time. As soon as a hog quit kicking he was heaved into the hogshead of scalding water and chounced up and down, head first, until the hair started to loosen. Then the men would pop the tail end in and chounce him some more. When the hair was good and loose they would haul him out on some boards and everybody began to scrape and pull hair to get it all off before it cooled.

Pap, being an extra good hand, always cleaned the feet and snouts while the common workers finished off the body. Then a gambrel stick was fastened under the whit-leather of the hind legs and the hog swung over a pole. Out came his insides into a tub. Then he was left to cool off, while the women stripped off the gut-fat, sorted out the livers and hearts, ground the sage, and got ready to make the sausage.

In three or four hours time, with some great fires roaring to heat water, steam whipping around in the cold so thick you could hardly see sometimes, the scalding, scraping, rinsing down and dressing was done and half a dozen great big hogs would be swinging by their hind legs, as naked as could be and white and clean as though they had never waded in a mudhole in their lives. They were allowed to hang there until after the evening chores were all done and supper over, then the job of cutting up began.

It was fun to see the men lay a big dressed hog on the table, flat on his back, spread his legs apart and cut him up. Off came his great head, out came the spare ribs, off came the hams, shoulders, sides, and all were trimmed up complete as could be. The scraps were thrown into a tub for later rendering into lard. When the cutting up was all done, the different parts were salted down and put away in barrels and boxes until dripping time came in the spring. The job of butchering was done again. It surely was a high spot in the winter line of sports.

When you hadn't had a bite of fresh meat for several months on end, that fresh pig liver, and heart, and tenderloin, tasted about as wonderful as anything that can be imagined. That, with spareribs and backbones, kept us mighty well fed for a good long time after the butchering was over.

It gives people a kind of comfortable feeling to have over two thousand pounds of pork laid away, to say nothing of pig's feet, and souse, and bags of sausage, and jowls for dandelion greens in the spring. The way we lived out there, there was always a lot put away to eat, and nobody ever went hungry.

Our smokehouse bulged with hams, shoulders, side meat, jowls and canvassed sausage, the finest you ever saw. The folks always packed the fresh pork in brine until along in the spring when they hung it in the smokehouse to drip for a week before it was smoked.

Then we chinked all the cracks, fastened down the window and started a smudge fire with hickory chips. In a short time the smokehouse got so smoked-up we had to either get out, or sneeze all the time. After that we went in only to put on more chips or put out a blaze.

We kept that up for two or three weeks. By that time the meat had turned brown on the outside and was just about too good to eat. Any kind of meat seemed good, but that smoked meat was always better than anything else, and there is no way of making anybody understand who never tasted it.

We had a wonderful cellar, too. The cellar itself wasn't anything to brag about, maybe, but what was in it is what I mean. There was a big bin at the back that held fifty bushels of apples. There were five sections to the bin, and each part had a different kind of apples in it. Some were to cook, and some were to just eat raw. Off to one side — in barrels — we always kept the snow apples and little red romanites, which were the best ones to take to school. There is nothing better, sort of in between times, than to gnaw an apple when you get a little tired of studying at school.

Over to one side in that wonderful cellar was a potato bin that must have held at least forty bushels. And there were places for beets, cabbages, onions, carrots, and all other kinds of garden truck, so that we never wanted for good things to eat all winter long. On the floor, at the right hand side of the door were five or six big jars of lard with cloths tied over them, while just back of them were a lot of pickles. There were cucumber pickles, tomato pickles, pickled apples, pickled pigs feet, and every other kind of spiced and fixed up goodie that you ever read about. Up on shelves sat rows and rows of canned fruits — cherries, plums, gooseberries, peaches, pears — put up in tin cans and sealed with wax. Sometimes a little of the wax would slip down into the fruit and make it taste a little off, but it was mighty good for all that.

There were a good many kinds of preserves down there, too. These were mostly put up in stone jars with a paper pasted over to keep the ants and cockroaches out. Once in a while a mouse or something would nibble a hole in the cover and cockroaches would get in there. It was a job to fish them out and generally Mother just threw the whole jarful away, and let it go at that.

Sometimes one of those soaking rains would come along and maybe last a week or so, and get the ground so soggy that water would seep into the cellar and stand a foot or two deep for a week or two. The planks that were laid down to walk on would commence to float around, and it was a wet job to go down there to get anything out. So Pap took a notion to put in a drain so as to always keep the cellar dry.

He had the boys dig a ditch as deep as the cellar was, leading away down through the apple orchard. He sent to the timber for four or five loads of poles, and dumped them in the ditch 'til it was nearly half full, and covered them up with dirt. It worked, too. After that there was never any more water backed up in the cellar, and we got along fine.

Between that wonderful cellar and all that was in it, and the smokehouse and all the lovely smoked meat in there, and a hogsheadful of sauer kraut, a pile of buried turnips, and a barrel of Silver Drip syrup, we never lacked for plenty to eat from the time the frost began to fly until pie plant time the next spring.

future farmers

It was a big day for us boys when we began to actually get a hand in the farm work — especially handling the horses. Horses are so big, and gentle, and brave, and strong. They are fast on foot, never get much tired of work — like people do — and they are not afraid of water, or mud, or the dark, or anything like that.

About the first thing a kid gets to do with horses

is to lead them out to the water trough to drink, then back to their stalls. After we had a few months of that, we were allowed to put a blind bridle on a trusty old mare and ride her to drive up the cows. We worked up a little at a time until the day finally came when we could actually hitch up a team to a plow and do work in the fields. That was what every country boy looked forward to.

I used to like to run the cornstalk cutter. It was a big red machine with two wheels, and underneath there was a set of great heavy knives that just naturally chopped the cornstalks to smithereens. I would drive, and drive, and drive that big team of smelly horses up and down the long corn rows all day long, and used to wave at everybody that went along the road to be sure that they saw me. Noontime was entirely too long, and one o'clock was welcome for that was when I got the horses out and hitched them to the cutter again. I was sorry when unhitching time came at night.

But following a harrow was a different story altogether. In those days nobody had ever thought of such a thing as rigging anything behind a harrow to ride on. The ground was soft as could be, and we sank into it halfway to our ankles every step. Of course we had some help from the lines but it got to be the most tiresome job you ever saw to wade across fields all day.

But there is an end to every day, and a boy rests up so fast that after a good night's sleep we were about as good as new and ready for another day of it, whatever it was we had to do. Farm work never hurt anybody and

we hadn't got to the worrying place yet. We were always having a good enough time in spite of our troubles.

The harvest season was about the finest of all. Cutting and binding the grain and setting it up in shocks all
over the field was as fine a thing to work at as we ever
had. And Pap had a way of keeping us at it — and keeping our interest up — with all kinds of baits.

One of these was "catching the rabbit." When the
reaper had cut off all four sides of the field a good ways
in, Pap would say, "It won't be long now 'til we catch
the rabbit." What he meant was that there was a rabbit
in every grain field, and when it came to cutting down
the last of it the rabbit would jump out and we would
get to chase him. I don't think we ever stopped to think
what we would do with the rabbit if we caught him.
They were no good to eat at that time of the year. I guess
it was just the natural hankering we had for chasing
something that is wild.

Putting up hay was a fine job too. Pap always drove
the mowing machine since he claimed to be a mechanic.
He made out that it took quite a genius to handle the
harvesting machinery.

Newly mown hay lying there in the sun — curing
for the stacks — has the most wonderful smell. There is
no perfumery that I ever ran across that comes up to it.
It was fun to pile it up with a horse rake, load it onto
wagons, and ride on top of it to the barn. Away up there
in the cool breeze it was mighty comfortable, with four
or five feet of loose hay underneath you — better than
any springs or cushions you ever read about.

Always looking for improvements to work with, Pap bought a new-fangled contraption called a hay carrier. A carrier on a long track, fastened up under the rafters in the haymow, carried the load back to where you wanted to dump it. The man on the load of hay would jab a scissors fork deep down in the hay and set it. Then he would give the word to Pete — the rope horse — who would start out away from the barn pulling on a great long rope that ran under the wagon, through several pulleys, up the far side of the barn, along the track and down to the hayfork.

Right away the load would begin to go up, pull loose from the main pile on the wagon, hit the carrier and go rattling back into the barn. The fork man held a little rope that was fastened to the fork and at the right time somebody in the mow would yell "Snack!" Then the fork man would give a little jerk and the whole pile would fall down into the mow. Eight or ten forkfuls would empty the wagon, and back to the field we would go for another load.

One thing that made haymaking a kind of skittish business was bumble bees. They get "ripe" about the same time hay does, and the work of putting up hay interferes with their plans. And they get mad about it, too. There isn't a particle of pacifism about a bumble bee. He doesn't know a thing about turning the other cheek. He is out for a fight the minute you disturb him.

Bumble bee colonies have only about a dozen bees in them. They build their nests in the ground, if they want to live in a hay field. Really it looks like they don't build nests at all, but steal them from mice and take them over for their own use. In these nests they will lay up the best honey that anybody ever saw. It isn't put up in any kind of comb, but is sealed up in little sacks about the size of a marble. Any kind of honey is mighty good to eat, but bumble bee honey is the best of all. It is sweeter, in the first place, and it has some kind of a flavor that seems to be made up of all the fine tasting things to be found out of doors. No wonder bumble bees are willing to defend their honey with their lives.

If you happen to shake up their nest any way, the whole colony of ten or twelve bumble bees will fly right into your face with the idea of stinging you right then. Unless you know your business, you are going to get stung, too. But we finally learned how to handle them and hardly ever got the worst of it.

One of the sports we used to like was "fighting out" bumble bee nests. Sometimes we found them in a hollow place around an old crib, and sometimes along a hedge row. The bees made nests almost any place they could find a mouse nest to steal. Generally three or four of us would go together to fight them, so as to help a fellow who might be getting the worst of it.

We would fix paddles out of shingles and stand all around the place where the nest was, 'til some one of us stirred it up. Out they would come, buzzing like everything and as mad as all get out. They would scatter out to take in all of us at once and we would swat them as they came on. Generally we would squash them all without getting a single sting. It was kind of ornery to gang on them that way, but it was safer.

Every acre or two of hay land had from one to three

bumble bee nests in it. When the mower passed over them they sometimes stayed stirred up and would sting the horses a little when they came around on the next swath. Then when the rake came along the next day and pulled their nest loose and scattered it around some, they got madder yet. By the time the wagon came along to pick up the hay, they were ready for the biggest kind of a fight.

But if you know how, you can catch every one of them in a jug as slick as you please. We tried the system and it worked fine. Take a jug half full of water and leave the cork out, and set it down right beside the nest. Then stir them up and run away before they can come out. Those fool bees will buzz around the top of that jug a few times and then flop right down into it and get drowned. They just seem to explore around the hole, then drop down in, tail first, and that is the last of them. By stirring them up several times, you can get the last one of them that way.

The first time we ever tried it Pap was mowing on a back lot not very far off, and along towards noon he got pretty dry for a drink of water. He wouldn't ask for a drink on a bet. He would do without for a whole week before he would ever admit that he was thirsty.

But Pap saw our bumble bee jug sitting out there in the open — with no one around — and walked over there to have a drink. We had no way of knowing what he was up to until he raised the jug to his mouth. Then it was too late. We jumped out from behind the hay-cock we were hiding in and yelled at him, but he didn't pay any attention to us. I'll bet there were a dozen half-drowned bumble bees in that jug of water. Pap spit out something and set the jug down. By that time we were pretty close to where he was, and trying to tell him about the jug. But it was no use saying what we knew. He scolded us a little for losing the corncob stopper, but never said a word about the bees. You never *could* figure him out at all.

Once a doctor in Burlington told him that the sting of bees was good for the rheumatism. It was the dead of winter, and the honey bees were all dormant and lazy as could be, all shut up in their hives. But he managed to get a handful somehow, then opened his shirt collar and poured that mess of bees right down his neck. Then he sat about in a warm room and waited for the bees to come to and sting him. After a while they began to crawl around inside his shirt, and one showed up under his ear, and he flicked it back inside as cool as you please.

He managed to get stung a good many times by those bees. He claimed they helped him, too. But mother raised a fuss about some of them that got loose in the house, because she was afraid they might sting the children. So Pap didn't get any more out of the hive, but just caught the strays he found buzzing around the house and put them inside his shirt front. There wasn't anything he was afraid of or wouldn't try if somebody recommended it to him.

At harvest time we used to trade work with the neighbors. Some of them didn't have harvesting machinery like we did, and they would help us through, and then we would go and help them.

We had a good many German neighbors and they

were the best of the lot — for they had a practice of eating five times a day at harvest time. On top of the three regular meals that other folks have, they would slip in one at half past nine in the forenoon, and another at half past three in the afternoon. The women folks would come out to the fields, lugging baskets full of sandwiches, radishes, onions, cheese, bologna, a big jug of buttermilk or something like that. We would all sit down on the ground and eat together. There was something to that kind of life. I always wished that I had been a German — but it was too late, and I always had to make out as I was. But I liked to work with those German neighbors, and eat and visit with them.

As a youngster, I never could understand Pap's talk about being glad for a bumper crop. I was always glad — especially after I got big enough to work steady in the fields — when there was a *short* crop of either small grain or corn. That made less work to do. Hard work and youngsters never did go well together, so I was always glad for a missing hill of corn at husking time and for the wet places where the grain had been drowned out. I was almost grown before I began to see that we had to depend on the crops for our living, our comforts and all our food.

passing of the prairie chicken

In my time back on Old Orchard Farm there used to be more wild prairie chickens than chickens of tame breeds. Nowadays I know a lot of people who have never seen a prairie chicken, for they have been gone from Iowa for many years.

But they used to be plentiful. It was one of the commonest things in the world to run onto a prairie chicken nest full of eggs. Like snipes, and many other birds, the mother hen tries to fool us to prevent us from finding her nest. Many times as I walked along in the grass, a prairie chicken hen would flutter right from under my feet with all the noise she could make, and fall on her side and squabble around in the grass just like she was crippled and could barely fly at all. I would run over intending to capture her alive, and just before I got my hands on her she would give a flounce and light fifteen or twenty feet away.

I would be right after her, expecting this time to make the capture. But she would be too quick for me, and away she would flutter — maybe hitting the ground several times before she came down to stay. Then I was sure she was tuckered out, and would run with all my might to pick her up. But when I was about three steps from her she would give two or three awkward flops and rise, maybe four or five feet from the ground, and fall forty or fifty yards away. By this means she would fool along with me for a good long way, and then fly off as fine as any prairie chicken you ever saw. It was a way they had of getting a person coaxed from their nests so that you never could find them again.

A prairie chicken hatches out a covey of fifteen or so young ones, and they are the cutest little things you ever saw, except young quails. Prairie chickens were used to the out of doors, and had good luck raising their young, so they multiplied to beat anything. Every grain field of forty acres in the country had a drove or two of chickens in it. All summer long you didn't see much of them, only by chance, for they lived mostly in the corn fields and weed patches. But after the small grain had been cut and shocked, they had a habit of coming out there to feed in the cool of the evening.

By August they were half grown, and the men used to go out after supper and hunt them. Two men would generally hunt together to cover more ground. Those chickens were mighty sly, and without a good hunting dog to find them you might just as well have stayed at home. During my first experience on this kind of a hunt I was too young to shoot a gun, so I just went along to carry the game.

John Cappes came over to our house and joined my big brother Joe and me for the hunt. John had borrowed a fine setter from a German named Henry Rawhert who had lived in this country only a short time and could just scarcely talk our language. But his dog seemed to understand everything the boys said to her.

Joe had a double barreled breech loader he had bought from Rawhert, who had set up a gunsmith shop on his farm down the lane. The left barrel was choke-bored and was made to get the game if you missed with the right barrel. That choke-bored barrel shot mighty close, and we had to be careful not to use it first or we might blow the game to pieces. Joe got a set of tools for reloading the brass shells, and these shells, when they were empty, had a smell about them that I liked better than almost any other smell. I used to help him reload on rainy days, by passing him the powder jar, or the shot sack, or the box of caps. I fully expected that some day he would let me shoot that wonderful gun. He did, too.

Early that evening of my first hunt we went out to the back oats field. The boys spread out about fifty feet apart, a short distance from the edge of the corn. The oats stubble was about eight inches high but many weeds had grown up since harvest and stuck up about a foot above the stubble in places. The dog was turned loose and went on ahead and away off to each side, and I trailed along behind.

We sauntered along that way for as much as a hundred yards or so, without finding anything to shoot. John Cappes allowed maybe it was a little too early in the evening. Joe was just starting to tell about a fine flock of young chickens he had seen in that very field earlier in the season when the setter stopped running, crouched down pretty low, and went crawling forward at a snail's pace.

I thought maybe she was getting tired or something. But the boys cocked their guns and got ready, for they said the dog was "setting game." It was all Greek to me. I had supposed that hunting dogs were used to catch game by running it down, like our blue dog did rabbits.

The setter stopped dead still, kind of crouched down, with her tail sticking out straight as a ramrod and one front foot lifted up. The boys walked a few steps closer. Then the setter went a little farther ahead, just creeping along. Then she came to a dead stop and wouldn't move a peg. We all slipped up to within a half dozen steps of her, and still she stood like she was paralyzed.

Then Joe gave her the word to "put it up." That meant, I soon saw, to scare the chicken out of the stubble so he could shoot. When he said this, that setter gave a forward spring, and out flew a fine young chicken. It flew up on John Cappes' side, so he shot, missing with the first barrel but bringing the chicken down with the second. I supposed that the hunt was all over, as no other birds flew up — and if there were any more there, I thought the crack of that gun would stampede them. But the dog stood like she was tied.

Joe motioned for the dog to go ahead, and she crept a few steps forward, while we all stood still and watched. Within ten seconds she came to another dead stop, and Joe again gave her the word. She sprang in and another chicken flew up. Joe downed it with his right barrel. Just then two other chickens came out of the stubble at the same time and the boys had a shot together. Joe missed with his right barrel, and then, taking plenty of time, he let that choke-bored barrel loose. The chicken fell seventy yards away.

That blessed setter dog worked back and forth all over that stubble, and one by one scared up about sixteen prairie chickens. It was a covey of an old hen and her brood. I don't remember how many the boys shot, but at least ten or eleven.

My first thought after four or five had been killed was what a job it was going to be to find all those dead chickens scattered all over the place for a hundred yards around. But to my surprise the dog did the work. As soon as the shooting was all over, Joe sent the setter out to bring in the game. The boys called this "retrieving." What surprised me was that the setter never stirred to go until she was told. She would go surging off, fast as she could run. I wouldn't think she could find anything at that pace, but all at once she would stick her nose down and bring up a chicken. Laying it down at our feet she would go at it again, 'til she had the last one of those chickens piled up. I thought that the German who had trained the dog must be a pretty smart fellow.

Some August evenings — especially if the weather was a little drizzly — we could hear guns booming in all directions, as the farmers brought down young prairie chickens by the hundreds. They never killed more than they wanted to eat, and we never could see that there were any fewer chickens the next year. Businessmen from Burlington, Mediapolis, and Morning Sun used to come out to hunt, for every farmer allowed hunting on his farm. There seemed to be no end of chickens.

But it was in the fall of the year that we saw real flocks of prairie chickens. When frost came and the fodder was shocked, with winter just around the corner, many coveys of prairie chickens joined forces. I have seen as many as a thousand in one flock. They sometimes came early in the morning and alighted on our barn, in the apple trees, and even on our house. A big walnut tree down in the field used to be a wonderful place for the chickens to light. I have seen that big tree so full of chickens that I couldn't see through it, and hundreds more would be on the ground.

Sometimes when we were shucking corn a great flock would come flying over and we could hear the whistling of their wings and see the stripes on their necks. They usually flew about fifteen or twenty feet above the ground and always in a straight line. It was a pretty sight in the dead of winter to happen onto a great flock of prairie chickens sitting on the snow and talking to one another in chicken language. I have seen whole hillsides literally covered with them.

Early in the spring they disbanded as great flocks and simmered down to little bunches, sometimes only two or three. During this season we heard them sing, if that is what to call it. It wasn't really much of a song, but sounded a whole lot like "Bum, bum, boo." Along between sundown and dark, in April or early May, we could hear them out in the pasture somewhere, "Bum, bum, boo; bum, bum, boo." And they would keep that up until after dark. Once I happened to be near enough a covey to discover that it was the roosters who sang. They seemed to swell up around the neck, put their heads back and do their "bum-booing" much like a tame rooster crows.

Several things contributed to wiping out the prairie chicken from the country fields. One thing was the passing of wild prairie grass, which was their natural home. Another was the improvement in guns. As long as the farmers had to load their guns by hand — from the muzzle — right out in the field, there wasn't a great deal of danger to the chickens. But when the time came that everybody had a breech loader or two, it was just too bad for all game birds.

The telegraph and telephone wires killed thousands. These wires were strung on poles about exactly the height that prairie chickens flew, and the poor things would fly right into them and break their necks. We boys found this out once when we went with Pap to a sale over in the Dode Miner neighborhood. Dode's boy took us out along the railroad and we found three or four dead prairie chickens lying right under the telegraph wires. Mother never would cook any of them for us, for she said you couldn't tell how long they had been dead. But we liked to find them anyhow.

Boys are not as particular about a lot of things as grown up people are. I remember once when a passel of us were exploring a marshy place that we found five or six big green frogs, about six inches long, sitting right on the edge of a pool. The water wasn't over a couple of inches deep, so we took after those frogs and caught them. Then one of the boys suggested that we kill them and skin them like they were Indians.

It was a pretty easy job to skin them. The meat was the whitest, prettiest looking meat you ever saw — looked good enough to eat. So we sent one of the boys back to his house to steal some matches and salt, built a fire, cooked those frogs' hind legs, and ate them. We all agreed frog legs were some of the finest meat we had ever tasted. We felt mighty guilty about it at the time and wouldn't have let the folks know about it for the world. But the time came when the same kind of frog legs would bring a quarter apiece in any good hotel.

We fried two ground squirrels once, on an old iron clock face fixed over some rocks, and they weren't so bad. One time Allen Lee shot a great big hawk over by his apple orchard, and we got it and cooked it. The meat was good enough, what there was of it, but awfully stringy and tough. Maybe we didn't get it cooked as much as it should have been, but it was nearly black when we ate it.

Once when we were coming home from school past Allen Lee's place we saw a rabbit sitting in a little brush heap at the lower end of his apple orchard. We sidled off, so as not to scare it, and ran back and told Allan about it. He got out his shotgun and came along with us, walking hunched away over with his knees bent forward long before we got near the rabbit. He crept to within two feet of the little brush pile, stuck the muzzle of that gun into it and whanged away.

When the smoke had cleared away we dug into the brush for our game, but all we could find of that rabbit was his ears, two paws, and some fur. That big charge, at so close range, had blown the poor bunnie into the next township, I reckon — maybe clear over as far as the insane asylum at Mount Pleasant.

That old asylum stood over across the prairie fifteen miles away. It spread out over several acres of ground and we could see the black smoke rolling out of its brick chimney when we looked over that way. People claimed it was full of crazy folks, and warned that if any of them ever got loose it would be a sorry day for us. With that great big solemn looking asylum looming up to the southwest, we never lacked something to tone us down if we ever got too gay.

When Pap took us over there to the asylum one Sunday, we found out that it wasn't such a bad place after all. The yard covered ten acres and was mowed as level as a floor. There was a pipe spouting up water in the middle of a little pond, and five or six geese jabbering around it. There were several benches out under the tall trees, and people were resting in them.

There were big rooms inside, and offices, and desks, and a place to register your name. A stairway six feet wide wound up and around to the upstairs, where I suppose the bedrooms were. After that I had a different feeling about the asylum.

At Fort Madison, another town only about forty miles from our house, there was a penitentiary. I could never muster up any notion of going down there, though. We never understood why our part of the state had both of these institutions so close together. Maybe we were more wicked and crazier than the rest of the state, but I doubt it.

The Mississippi River was only eighteen miles east of us, and in wet times, got to be several miles wide. It was one of the grandest sights you ever saw. When some smart aleck came along and got to bragging about the wonders of his part of the country, we used to be comforted by *our* Fort Madison penitentiary, the Mount Pleasant insane asylum and the Mississippi River.

"clair away the dogs, I'm a comin'"

Between grain harvesting and thrashing there was a slack time for a few days and nearly everybody took a kind of "lay off." Sometimes we went to the Mississippi for a fishing trip, sometimes bee hunting in the timber, and sometimes just "lazed" around the place and rested up. For several years Pap mentioned taking us all to the woods for a coon hunt. But something always happened — like a new job, or Pap with fresh rheumatism, or something. But one year we did go.

We had two good dogs, one named John Tyler and the other John Carler. They were regular hounds, with great long ears and a sad look in the face. When George Brown got ready to move to Missouri he gave us a young hound he had bought from a peddler for a silver dollar. This dog was about half grown, just big enough to worry the life out of the old dogs, woozling them around and never giving them a chance to sleep. Pap decided a coon hunt would be good training for the young dog.

One evening a light drizzle struck up about sundown, and Pap said it was just the time to track a coon. So just as it was getting dark we loaded the dogs into the big wagon, piled in, and drove about five miles south, deep into the big woods. We tied the horses to a tree and turned the hounds loose. They went sniffing off into the dark and we wanted to follow them, but Pap made us stay at the wagon 'til the dogs struck a trail. It was as dark as Egypt. We sat there, hardly saying a word, hoping to hear from the dogs.

Within fifteen or twenty minutes we heard old John Tyler let out a bawl, and John Carler joined in. Pap lit the lantern and away we went, as fast as we could through the hazel brush and fallen trees, in the direction of the sounds. We had a lot of faith in Pap's woodsmanship and weren't much scared of getting lost, but we couldn't see our hands before us if we turned down the lantern wick. We went down a long hill, crossed a running creek, and climbed up a clay bank that was so steep and slick that we had to help one another up. Then we stood still awhile, for the dogs were nearly out of hearing over another big hill and Pap said they would circle back our way.

After a while we could notice the sounds were getting closer, and pretty soon they sounded like they were only about a hundred yards off, and coming right toward us. We asked Pap if a coon would bite anybody, and he told us no, not if we didn't bite the coon. We kept our eyes peeled but didn't see anything of him. We couldn't even see the dogs when they went by.

There may be more exciting sounds than hounds bawling on a hot trail, but I have never heard any. Both old dogs were going it to beat anything, and by that time the young dog had learned how, and was bawling as loud as the others. They trailed that coon away off to the northwest, and then we heard them to the east, coming down the hill on the other side of the creek. So we took after them as fast as we could go, with Pap ahead carrying the lantern and pointing out the rocks and logs so we wouldn't break our fool necks.

Sometimes there would be a lull in the bawling, and Pap said they had lost the trail. We felt disappointed about that, but pretty soon they would find it again and set up a bigger yelping than ever. That coon was a smart one and kept a comfortable distance ahead of the dogs most of the time. When they got too close he waded in the creek for several rods, and the dogs had trouble finding where he came out. That gave him a fresh start.

At last, they treed him — about nine o'clock. **Pap** knew right away by the change in the sound the hounds made. On the trail they had given out a long bellow — like they were crying about something — but now they barked in short loud yelps.

When we got there all the dogs were squatted under a great big oak tree, looking up and barking.

Pap set the lantern down and went over and put his ear against the side of the tree, and listened. We asked him what he was doing, and he told us he wanted to find out whether it was a coon or a bear. That made us shake in our boots a little, but we believed Pap could kill a bear barefisted if he had to, so we didn't say anything. Pretty soon he straightened up and allowed it was a coon, and went to work to "moon" him, as he called it.

He put the lantern on top of his head and went around the tree, looking at every limb slowly and carefully. Finally he saw the coon on the first limb, which ran about forty feet out and twenty feet up. Then Pap let us "moon" him. Sure enough, there he was — a big fat coon right over our heads and not a chance in the world to get away. We started in to cut down that tree with the short handled axe we had carried along. It was certainly a whopper of a tree. It must have been close to four foot through at the butt, with bark rough as could be. After taking turns for half an hour or so we didn't have more than the bark off one side, and were pretty well winded. Then Pap took a hand, but complained that the axe was a woman's size, and pretty soon he quit. We calculated that it would take a week to cut that tree down with such an axe, so Pap said he would climb up and shake the coon down.

Pap was a wonderful climber. He was raised in the big timber and had climbed hundreds of big trees. He was strong as a horse and wasn't afraid of anything. He took off his boots and started up the tree. We stood watching for forty minutes or more as Pap inched his way up. Several times he stopped to rest, but he never said a word about being tired. After a long time he got to that first limb, and lapped his fingers around it. But he was too tuckered out to pull himself up on top the limb. So after resting a minute or two he swung himself out into the dark and went overhanding it toward the coon. He looked kind of scary up there, with his long legs dangling down. The dogs were whooping it up, anxious to get a tooth into that coon.

When Pap got out about twenty-five feet he tried to get on top of the limb. Once he got a leg up within a few inches of the limb, but couldn't make it, and had to let down again. He was a heap more fagged than he would admit, and had to give up. Then we heard him say, kind of solemn, "Boys, I believe I better get back to the tree. I'm give out."

We tried our best to get him to go on and shake the coon down. But he knew better than we did and started to overhand it back toward the trunk. We hated to lose that coon after having almost caught him. Before Pap got ten feet along that limb, he stopped and hung there like he was resting. Then we heard him say, "I'm never goin' to make it. I'm give out."

We were scared then, and warned him that it was twenty feet or more to the ground, too far to drop. But it wasn't any use. He was at the end of his rope.

"Clair away the dogs. I'm a comin'."

Before we could any more than get our hands on their collars, he came thrashing down among us. A big hazel bush helped break his fall, but he hit the ground with an awful thud.

Too excited to think, we let the hounds loose. They pounced right onto Pap, bellowing and snarling. The young dog was the worst. He sure did spread himself.

"Take 'em off! Take 'em off!" Pap yelled, all curled up there in the dim light of the lantern, about as near helpless as I ever saw him.

"Pap," Joe answered, "if you could grin and bear it a little longer, it would be the makin' of the young dog."

But in the general scramble and noise, I don't think Pap ever heard the remark. The old dogs soon discovered their mistake and went back to barking up the tree. The young dog, not knowing what else to do, let loose of Pap's britches and went to barking at the tree too.

Pap was considerable "stove up" in his legs and had a gash under one eye where he had hit the hazel bush. But we got him into the wagon, and he drove home. He rubbed a lot of spavin cure all over himself and took a big dose of National Kidney and Liver Cure and went to bed. In a day or two he was all right as far as anybody could see. He was a tough one.

We didn't sleep three winks all night, thinking about that coon. Lying there wide awake as owls, we planned it all. Next morning at daybreak we were back at that tree, with two good axes and all three dogs. There, at the end of that limb was a big squirrel nest that we had all taken for a coon the night before. It was an awful disappointment not to get that coon.

But we were worse than disappointed in Pap. We had supposed that he could do anything in the world he ever tried, and we hated to find out it wasn't so. But, of course, we never spoke a word to him about it. To do that would have taken a hundred times more grit than any of us had.

a trip to the mill

We raised all our own wheat in those days on Old
Orchard Farm. We hardly ever sold any of it, because
it took most of it to keep our big family. Mother always
baked our own bread, of course. The kind she baked
was mighty good, too, so we ate a lot of it three times
a day. In winter we generally had buckwheat cakes for
breakfast, with ham gravy or sorghum molasses. But

wheat bread was the main standby, so we raised wheat for that.

Though our folks usually went to the grist mill at Kossuth, there were others at Lowell and New London. The Kossuth mill was a couple of miles closer, and some claimed that they didn't take quite as much toll.

It was a pretty place down around that mill, with a fine big creek running right past it and a spring of good water. It was a full day's trip there and back from Old Orchard Farm, so the men always took their dinner and feed for the horses. It was a trip which took us over into Yellow Springs township, ten miles or more, with a whole day with nothing to do but just jog along the road and laze around the mill, waiting for the grist.

When I was twelve years old I begged Mother to ask Pap if I could go along to the mill on the next trip. I hadn't started to work in the fields, so except for pulling weeds, carrying water, herding the cattle, driving flies, bugging potatoes, picking berries, and helping with the chores, I didn't have much to do. Pap wasn't much for the idea at the start. He asked why I wanted to go and wondered if I just wanted to get out of work. But Mother told him that I had been a good boy, had never been anywhere much, and that it wouldn't hurt to let me go. Pap never said I could or couldn't, so Mother told me to count on going. She said that if Pap didn't want me to go he wouldn't be a bit backward about saying so.

So we could get an early start on the day of the trip we always sacked the grain the night before. Usually we took six sacks of wheat and two sacks of corn. We always welcomed corn cakes as a change from the wheat cakes, so Pap raised some white corn which we shelled for that purpose. After supper the men brought four or five hundred ears of white corn into the kitchen, got down a tub or two, a dishpan, and a couple of buckets. Then we gathered around to shell corn.

Shelling corn required a special technique which we quickly learned. We took a corn cob and shelled off three or four rows down the side of the ear, then with the thick part of the palm and with a twisting motion we shoved the kernels toward that open part on the cob until they broke loose to fall into the pile. That method worked well at first, but after shelling a dozen ears or more a blister often showed up on our hands, forcing us to use a corn cob to shell with for the rest of the evening. It was slower, but by ten o'clock we usually had about four bushels, which would make a lot of meal.

That trip to the mill was one of the finest experiences I ever had. We rode along perched up on the spring seat, with a sheepskin for a cushion, behind a fine team of horses, with a big umbrella to keep the sun off. We saw people all along the roadside doing the commonest kinds of work right out in the glare of the sun, while we seemed detached from the world, riding in luxury.

We passed the Tucker farm, the Michaels' place, and the Michaels' school, painted red. The first thing I knew we were out of our neighborhood and passing the place where Henry Fye lived. He was the one who owned the thrashing machine. It wasn't long then 'til we came to

the Shortridge place, where they made sorghum molasses.
There was the sweep, the furnace, the vats, and a big
stovepipe most fifty feet high which had to be held
straight up by wires tied toward the top and fastened to
posts around it. I couldn't figure out how anybody ever
got up there to fasten those wires.

Pretty soon we came to Flint creek, but at first it was
pretty much of a disappointment to me, since I had
heard a lot about Flint creek and supposed it was as big
as a river. Joe explained that where we crossed it was
pretty well up, and that down below a few miles it was
a lot bigger. I was glad to hear him say that. A fellow
doesn't like to find wonderful things smaller than he
thought they were.

In another half hour we drove right along in front
of the Linn Grove churches, sitting there in the woods,
nearly surrounded by gravestones. My hair practically
stood on end, for I had often heard the folks tell about
the Linn Grove churches. I had always wanted to see
them, and there they were right before my eyes!

They stood about a hundred yards apart. One of
them was built of bricks and the other was a frame
church. About every Sunday services were held in the
frame church, but the brick one hadn't had a sermon
preached in it since the big fight twenty years before.
Some trouble over the war had caused bad blood between the neighbors and it all came to a head at the
dedication, with a big, general fight in which two or
three were killed and several more crippled for life.
That was the end of that church for good and all. It

was never used but the one time. After six or seven years, some of the neighbors built the frame church, and just let the brick one stand there empty. It had the same coal oil in the lamps, the same Bible still lay there on the pulpit, all mildewed over, and several of the benches were scattered around, just like they lay after the fight. Weeds and grass had grown up around the sides and along the stone walk. It was one of the most dismal looking churches anybody ever saw.

People claimed to have seen lights in that church in the night, but when they investigated there wouldn't be any lights at all. Some claimed it was rowdies trying to scare people, but the general belief was that the brick church was haunted. Mighty few people would venture past there in the night alone.

My brother Bob was riding along there one night, going home from seeing his girl, and was stopped right in the middle of the road by two men with pistols in their hands. He socked his spurs into his horse's sides and rode right through them; then he took out his twenty-two revolver and shot back in their direction as long as his seven loads lasted.

We got to Kossuth about eleven that morning, turned several corners among a lot of little cottages, and drove down the long clay hill, with the brakes so tight that both hind wheels were sliding. All at once we came to the mill, and a minute later drove right under a portico and stopped by the unloading door.

Joe seemed to know where to go without asking any questions. The miller came to greet us and receive the grist. He was dressed all in white, with a little white cap on his head and flour all over his face and hands. They had some funny looking little wheelbarrows that stood right up on end, with little round iron wheels not much bigger than a silver dollar. A sack of grain just exactly fitted on them, and one by one, ours were taken off and wheeled into the mill. The miller waved his hand and Joe drove the team around behind the mill, where there was the prettiest kind of an open place, right beside the creek. We unhitched the horses, tied them to the wagon box and gave them their oats and hay. Then we went into the mill to look around.

It was one of the most wonderful places I had ever seen. As we went by the power house we looked in there and saw the big steam engine that ran the whole mill. What fooled me was that it didn't make any more noise than a bobsled. There was a flywheel twenty feet across, going round and round. Right back of the engine was the boiler room where a man with the dirtiest face I ever saw was shoveling coal into a roaring furnace. I got kind of shaky in there for I had heard you never could tell when a steam boiler might blow up.

In the mill almost everything was out of sight. We looked through some little glass doors on the sides of the machines and saw the rollers, shakers, sifters, and all kinds of machinery at work. But everywhere we looked there were great big leather belts whizzing around, and a humming noise going on that made it hard to understand anything that was said. After a while the miller came around and took us all over the mill, up narrow stairsteps, through dark halls, and even up to the fourth story, where we could look right down on the horses. They didn't look much bigger than colts.

Afterwards we went down to the wagon and ate our dinner. Mother was a great hand to fix up a cold snack — we had chicken, cucumber pickles, beets, lots of bread and butter, some apple sauce, a jug of sweet milk with the cream left on, and some raspberry pie. After dinner we rolled up our britches and waded in the creek for about an hour, over smooth rocks that were as much as ten feet across. We got down and drank out of the big spring, but we had drunk so much milk at dinner that we weren't very thirsty.

Then we took a stroll around the town, and soon found out that there wasn't much to Kossuth except the mill. People said it had been a sizeable place once, but the railroad was built through two miles west, and a town had sprung up that they called Mediapolis. This was hard on Kossuth. But it was still an interesting place.

Along about two o'clock the miller motioned that the grist was ready, so we hitched up and drove around to the delivery door. Soon the sacks were loaded and we were off for home. We had to go through the middle of Mediapolis, and got to give that town a looking over. We had passed through it on the way down, but I was so excited about getting to the mill that I hadn't paid any attention to it.

We got another look at the haunted church as we drove back through Linn Grove. We met old Ben "Peg-leg" Ward right in front of it. He was sitting there in his buggy when we drove up, taking a good look. He ran a little restaurant and pool hall at Yarmouth, and we knew him pretty well. It was nice to see somebody from home when we were so far away.

Of course talk turned right away to the haunted church, and Old Ben allowed there wasn't the slightest doubt about it, for several times he had seen lights in that church. Once he saw men hanging to the beams away up under the eaves, but when they noticed him they all let go and thrashed right down into the ground and didn't show up again. He allowed they were dead folks from the graveyard who had crawled up there to cool off and skedaddled when anybody saw them. It sounded reasonable enough to me, but Joe told me on the way home he didn't take much stock in such talk.

Then Old Ben told us a regular hair-raiser about an experience he had at that haunted church about a year before. He said he was driving past about an hour after midnight. The sky was as clear as a bell and the moon was shining as bright as day. As he got right in front of the graveyard he heard a moaning sound and stopped his team to listen. He didn't hear anything more for a minute or so, then it set in again, same as before. Sounded, he said, like it came from away down deep somewhere, but he couldn't make out just where.

So he climbed out and went over into the graveyard and looked around. Some white owls flew off into the timber, and a skunk crawled out of the grass and slinked under the woodshed, but outside of that he said he didn't see a sign of life, just gravestones all around.

Pretty soon he heard a "Baa-a-a-a, ba-a-a-a-a-a" that sounded like a sheep in a well or something. He stumbled around the place, he said, and finally came to an open grave that hadn't been used yet, and peeked in to see what was there. It was a tolerable deep grave, he said, but by getting down on his hunkers he could make out some white object. It gave out another "Baa-a-a-a," and Pegleg knew he was on the right track.

And then Old Ben told us something pretty hard to believe. He told us that he shoved a pole down into that grave and slid down to satisfy himself what kind of a "hant" it was that could blatt that way. All he found was just a sheep. A whole flock of them pastured in the graveyard, and one had fallen into that grave and couldn't get out.

Old Ben said he spent the balance of the night trying to climb that pole, but every time his wooden leg would catch on something and down to the bottom he would go. He had the inside of the grave all punched full of holes trying to hold what he had gained by jabbing his wooden leg into the side walls. He stayed in that grave he said, 'til almost noon the next day before he was able to make anybody hear him. The first two or three people who came that way, "broke and ran like the devil was after them" when they saw his hat sticking out of that grave. Finally, he said, Old Joe Mussack, who was never afraid of anything, came by on his way to the mill and hauled Pegleg out.

Maybe it was so, and maybe it wasn't. But I never saw the time even after I grew up, when I could go past the Linn Grove churches in the night without feeling kind of creepy.

We got home from the mill about sundown. The men carried the sacks into the smokehouse, emptying them into nice clean barrels, while Mother pressed the flour down with her hands and filled them all to the brim. Then she put a round lid on every barrel, and a rock on top — to keep out the rats and chickens.

I was in a daze for a week or two, until the glory of that wonderful trip began to wear off. It was the finest trip a boy ever took, it seemed to me. Right from the time we drove out of the barnlot through the whole stretch of twenty miles there and back, it was just one exciting sight after another. And that double-barreled look we got of the Linn Grove churches, and what Old Ben Ward told us, was enough to satisfy any reasonable boy for almost a lifetime.

I tried to tell the Conkling boys about it, but they weren't much impressed. They had been as far as Kingston, six or seven miles the other side of Kossuth, and in a week were going to Wapello, in another county. They had been past the Linn Grove churches many times, and had seen as many ghosts as a dozen at a time.

But it was good enough for me. That trip to the mill was all I ever expected it to be — and a whole lot more. If I could be a boy again and were told by the President that I could pick out one thing to do that I would rather do than anything else in the world, I wouldn't stutter a bit in choosing to go to Kossuth to the mill with my big brother Joe.

yorknuts and puppy love

I have heard a lot of talk about the lonesome and drab sort of life people live out in the open country. But a whole lot of that talk is just bunk. As far as we were concerned, we had just the bulliest kind of times all the year round.

For one thing, I never used to hear anybody complain much about times being hard, or money tight.

During the time I was growin' up at Old Orchard Farm
I don't believe people were much excited about making
money. All they seemed to want was just a comfortable
living. If we had good crops, we had a good living that
year. If the crops were short, we cramped down a little,
but got along somehow. We always had plenty to eat
and wear. Nothing gaudy, of course, or particularly
stylish, but good enough.

Pap never had a thought of money grubbing, I am
sure. He got a stump patch in Brown county, Illinois,
when his father died, and a few years later he traded
that, even up, for a quarter section of mostly raw land in
Iowa. By always keeping out of debt he generally had
money in his britches pockets, and sometimes, after selling off a herd of hogs, would have as much as two or
three hundred dollars to carry around. He never thought
of getting robbed.

But Pap hung on to his money. He didn't hand
it out to any of his kids. We went without a cent from
one year to the next. One Fourth of July, when I was
fourteen or fifteen years old, I went to New London —
ten miles away — on horseback, with a silver dime in
my pocket and a lunch done up in a rag. Mother had
given me the dime — from a dozen eggs she sold for the
purpose, for Pap never thought of anything like that.

First I bought a glass of red lemonade at the celebration and got a nickel back in change. Along in the afternoon I blew the balance of my wealth for a sack of fresh
roasted peanuts, which I nibbled at for a couple of
hours. After they were gone I wanted a drink of lemon-

ade worse than ever, but my money was all gone. So I went over to the town pump in the middle of the public square and got a big drink of water. I went without any supper because I wanted to stay for the fireworks, then rode home in the dark. I got there about ten o'clock. Mother was awake listening for me, but Pap was sound asleep as a possum. Nothing worried him.

Another Fourth of July, when I was about sixteen, we were all going to Linn Grove, down on Flint creek. But I had been jumping in my Sunday boots and busted one of them all to pieces, and Mother was worried what to do about me. I was too big to go barefooted, and my feet were so big I couldn't wear any of the girls' work shoes. It was awful to think of staying home on the Fourth of July. But Belle thought up something that saved the day for me. She got the idea I was to wear the good boot I had and bind up the other foot like it had been cut or injured.

So that is what I did. When we got there I climbed out of the wagon and started to walk into the grounds just like nothing had happened. But Belle stopped me and said, "You got to limp with that sore foot. No, not so much as that. Just a little, so it will look natural like." So I cut a cane from a sumac bush, and limped a little with my bandaged foot. Lots of folks from our neighborhood asked me what had happened to me. But I always shrugged it off with a casual "Nothing much," and let it ride that way. It was a bully idea and I was always thankful to Belle for thinking it up.

We had an old lake bed on our farm that used to

be big enough to cover ten acres seven or eight foot deep with water. But after all the fields around were plowed up, the water washed so much dirt in when big rains came that it got badly shallowed up. Finally cattle got to bogging down in there and the lake had to be drained out by digging a big ditch out of the lower end. After that a creek was all that remained.

Lillies had been growing along the shallow parts of that lake for goodness knows how long, and they had big pods of nuts on them that our folks called yorknuts. The nuts looked like hazel nuts in size and color, but were as round as buckshot. They had a thin, tough shell and the meat was as hard as a rock. We thought their little green hearts were poisonous so we always picked them out before eating the meat.

When I was a boy, that lake had been drained for several years, but we could still find yorknuts after a big rain. One of our favorite sports was to roll our britches up to our knees and go yorknut hunting down at the lake bed. Boys used to come for miles around to hunt them. And so did girls, but mostly they never found any, so we divided ours with them.

Twenty years after any yorknuts had grown in that lake, we could still find a good many where the creek bank crumbled off. There the little brown balls would be sticking in the mud, half buried in the bank and shining like everything. They were just as hard and as good as ever.

In the wintertime we had get-togethers such as spelling bees and literary societies about every week.

We used to ride horseback as far as Liberty schoolhouse, six miles away, to go to one.

Stella Walker, at White Cloud, was our champion speller. She was the cutest little thing, with black eyes and lips that always looked moist and inviting. It seemed to me she could spell any word in the world, and she didn't have to study, either. I got so interested in Stella that I used to ride all the way to her house alongside her horse on the way home. It was out of the way some, but I didn't mind that.

As time went on I found myself thinking about her a good deal of the time, and finally I asked if I could come to see her. Not long after that I borrowed a top buggy from John Cappes and took her to a celebration at New London on the Fourth. I had forty cents and she had a quarter, so between the two of us we had all the treats we needed. Her mother furnished the dinner for us, and I took along a dozen Early June apples.

We drove home after the fireworks — just the two of us — and it was as pleasant as could be. I just let the horses walk the whole ten miles, and she never complained a bit. I tried a few words of spelling on her, but I couldn't think of very many. Then we talked about what a pretty night it was, and the stars, and what good times we always had at school. When I let her out at the front gate I asked for a lock of her hair. She asked me if I had a knife but I didn't, so I had to drive off without the lock of hair.

When Ed Conkling came back from working in the

scraper factory at Mount Pleasant, he had a lot of new fangled ideas he had picked up from the town boys and a brand new top buggy of his own. He started going with Stella and I lost out. But I always liked her anyway, and never saw her afterwards without feeling a little like I did that night on the way home from the celebration.

Our Friday night literary societies were a mixture of recitations, papers, essays, a recess, and a big debate. Nearly everybody in the neighborhood went to them except Joe Mussack and Tom Darbyshire. Sometimes the meetings lasted half the night. We debated about whether "Fire Is More Destructive Than Water," "The Pen Is Mightier Than the Sword," "Republics Are Better Than Monarchies," and "Webster Was Greater Than Clay." We never touched on politics or religion since none of us knew anything about either one of them, anyhow.

I got my first start in public speaking at these literary societies. Dave Michaels was the one that egged me on after I thought I had made a mess of my first appearances. Dave said he always knew I was good for something besides carrying swill to the pigs. This perked me up, and I kept on trying 'til I got so I could get along pretty well.

We had wonderful times at our play parties, too. These came off during the winter, always at somebody's house. We never had a fiddler to play for us, like a regular dance, but several of the boys played French harps, and all of us could bend a paper over a comb and hum through it. For some of the turns we sang the music. One of our favorites was "Skip to My Lou":

> My wife's left me, skip to my Lou,
> My wife's left me, skip to my Lou,
> My wife's left me, skip to my Lou,
> Skip to my Lou my darling.

Then one of the girls in the ring would bounce out toward one of the boys she wanted to dance with. He would meet her more than half way, slip his arm around her waist, and they would go circling around to the music. Then the words changed to:

> Gone again, skip to my Lou,
> Skip to my Lou my darling.

Then the fellow who had just lost his partner would begin:

> I'll get another one, sweeter than you,
> I'll get another one, sweeter than you,
> Skip to my Lou my darling.

Then he would step out and motion to the girl he wanted to dance with and she would meet him, and they would go circling around, too. After a bit we all danced at the same time and kept it up 'til the harp players got blisters on their mouths keeping up the music.

When we got tired of that we would sit down and

play "Simon Says Thumbs Up," or "Fox and Geese," to rest up. Then away we would all go again on:

Charlie he's a nice young man,
Charlie he's a dandy,
Charlie likes to kiss the girls,
Because it comes so handy.

Over the river to water my sheep,
Over the river to Charlie,
Over the river to see the gay widow,
And measure up my barley.

I don't want any your weevily wheat,
I don't want any your barley,
It takes the very best of wheat,
To bake a cake for Charlie.

On and on we went, making up verses as we went along. We danced first with one girl and then another 'til we had made the rounds three or four times. It was the pleasantest way in the world to get acquainted and spend an evening. Anybody could see that.

Then some lovesick girl would say, "Let's play Post Office," or "Needle's Eye," or "Drop the Handkerchief." Some of our crowd always seemed to like to play those kissing games best of all. I never complained about them myself.

These play parties got to be so popular that we had one almost every week. My sisters and I used to ride horseback as far as five or six miles in the coldest kind of weather to attend them. And sometimes we got home away after ten o'clock. Once at Doctor Baldwin's house in Yarmouth, after the Doc and his woman had yawned around for an hour or so, along about ten he said, "Sarah, I guess we better go to bed; I think these youngsters want to go home." But we told him we weren't in any particular hurry to go, and stayed nearly another hour. It was young love at work, and we hated to part company.

But after a while some of the grown up boys got to coming. They brought whiskey with them, and that led to trouble and a good many fights. Parents wouldn't let their girls go any more, and it about broke up our play parties. After that some of us tried going to the regular dances, where they had a regular fiddler, but we never had as much fun as we did at our old affairs.

In the wintertime we made sleds to coast down hills and had some wonderful times. This was especially fine sport when we could get a girl to ride down the hill with us. Girls never could learn to guide a coaster without busting into something or turning the sled upside down. We generally had to put them on the front of our sleds and pilot them down the big slick hill ourselves. Sometimes we would make a mistake and go sliding off into the deep snow and maybe upset, going faster than a horse could run. But that was a lot of fun and we never had a really serious accident.

We skated sometimes, but we never had any "store skates" so it didn't amount to much. About all we could do was slide along on our boot soles, so we didn't keep it up very long and our "skating" never got to be as popular as coasting.

When we got old enough to do some real sparking we had dozens of bobsled rides — whole parties of six or seven couples going together in a wagon box half filled with straw. We'd have a spanking team of horses strung over with sleigh bells that jingled in the frosty air. Then we snuggled down in the straw, wrapped in bed quilts and horse blankets so we kept warm as could be.

Those really were the times and I surely remember them. The jingling sleigh bells with a music all their own — the prancing horses with their breath sending up clouds of steam in the frosty night air — your best girl snuggled close at your side — all of these put together made a pleasant evening every time. We never felt any worries about entertainment for country lads and lasses, and I'll bet a lot of the town kids would envy us.

revival

at

head

of

flint

church

We boys always wanted to visit the Head of Flint
Church when a revival meeting was on, but Pap would
not let us go. He said there was a rough crowd down
there and we might get into trouble. That made us
want to go worse than ever. Head of Flint, a Wine-
brenarian church five or six miles south of our house,
sat on a hillside near the headwaters of Flint creek,

from which it got its name. One winter Pap got elected to serve on the grand jury, so we just up and went to visit Head of Flint one night. We picked a good night, for they had one of the biggest times that night they ever had.

In those days no protracted meeting was any good without testimonies. When that part of the service was ordered, the folks began to get up — one after another — and tell their religious experiences. Some of these were plum whoppers, but these folks had told them so often they believed them, so we didn't hold it against them.

The night we went to Head of Flint, Alex Sheppard gave his experience, and went into the thing in dead earnest. "It was twenty-three years, six months, and four days ago, when I was a choppin' wood out in the timber, all alone, and the Spirit came along and lep' on me like a dog. I tried to git away and keep on in my sins, but was overcome by the Spirit, and laid there 'til the folks found me, all out of my head and feverish, and carried me home. I have been under the blood ever since, brothers, and washed as white as any wool you ever saw."

Just then some mischievous fellow broke in and asked him if he didn't mean as white as dog's hair. He said that if Alex started in likening the Lord's spirit to a dog, he ought to stay with it, hair, hide, tail, and all.

Then a lot of crazy talk started and as many as twenty men and a few women got mixed up in it. Aunt Sarah Armstrong started to sing, and Old Noddy Brooks jumped up on a seat and yelled, "Let us pray!" About that time somebody kicked the stovepipe down. Smoke began pouring out into the room, setting everybody to coughing and sneezing, 'til they had to open the windows to get their breath. It was nearly zero weather and the wind blew out all the coal oil lamps. The women began to scream, and the children started to cry. Everybody edged toward the doors to go home and the meeting ended right then and there.

Outside, the Lowell fellows got to quarreling with some of the Head of Flint crowd. Soon they got into a fight, and several of them had black eyes, peeled noses, and were generally bunged up. It was an awful thing to happen at church, and we thought it would end the revival for good. It didn't, though, and the next night there was a bigger crowd than ever. Experiences were told that outdid Alex Sheppard's by a good ways. Pierkses two boys were there and told us afterwards that if anything ever happened to them like the things the Head of Flint folks bragged about the Lord doing, they would never quit running as long as they had a breath in them. But we had all we wanted of Head of Flint and never went back. Anyway, Pap would have made it warm for us if he ever found out.

But the bulliest place of all to attend a meeting was at Trinity Church, three miles west of our house. It was a Primitive Methodist crowd, with more "religion" to the square inch than anybody I ever saw. It was better than a circus and never cost a cent.

Every night at a protracted meeting the house would

be jammed to the doors, with a lot standing outside looking in the windows. The service generally would start off with singing five or six songs, followed by a season of prayer. Many of these prayers had been learned by heart and were rattled off without a break. Others seemed to be made up as they went along, and were pretty poor. Sometimes two would get to praying at once, and maybe before they got through a third and fourth one would join in, and you couldn't understand a thing that was said. Old Brother Cartman said the Lord could understand even if everybody felt moved to pray at once. We always doubted that a little.

After another song or two, the preacher would name a text and preach a short sermon, made up mostly of exhortations calling for people to repent of their sins and turn to the Lord. Pretty soon the working members would get enough of that and start up a song, and people were begged to come to the altar for prayers. A dozen or so of the old standbys would go forward and drop down on their knees at the mourners' bench, and start to pray as loud as they could talk. Then for half an hour or so — between singing, praying, exhorting, and all — a dozen or so passed through the congregation hauling at the folks to get them to the altar. Lots of folks did go forward every night, and the workers labored with them, as they called it, trying to "bring them through."

Along about ten o'clock somebody would jump up from the mourners' bench and yell out "I've got it, I've got it," maybe six or seven times in a row.

"Amen, amen, amen," would come from all over the

front part of the church. Then somebody would start
to jump up and down, and some more would join in
right away, and they would shout and hug one another
like they were tickled most to death. They would flock
around the new convert as thick as flies, and shake his
hand and pound him on the back, and say, "Glory halle-
lujah, praise the Lord!"

Then about that time another one would "come
through" and more people would shout and clap that
one on the back. Pretty soon there would be a general
breaking out — like the measles — and every member
would be singing, or shouting, or praying, or exhorting,
or prancing around the aisles, until they got worked up
to a regular frenzy. We tried not to miss anything but
it was a tough job, for there was so much going on all
the time that a person needed two or three pairs of eyes
to take it all in.

Along about eleven o'clock somebody started what
they called "the Holy Pilgrimage," kind of a grand
march up and down the aisles and around the church.
This marching never seemed to interfere with the half
dozen other things doing on. Everybody did whatever
popped into his head, and it got to be a regular picnic.
By that time several of them would be in a trance, flat
on the floor, limp as a rag, their eyes set and just plum
gone. That was held to to be the farthest anybody
could go in grace, but it never seemed like much to me.
Then their families carried them out to the bobsleds and
took them home. The doxology ended the meeting 'til

the next night, when they would all be back at it as hard as ever.

But Trinity Church never got any bigger, because these converts nearly all backslid during the summer and fall to furnish the timber for the next revival to work on. They joined church every winter as sure as there was a revival. And their joining, even the fourth or fifth time, seemed to tickle the working members just as much as ever. Nobody ever seemed to question the sincerity of their antics.

Our family never got mixed up in those meetings except as spectators. For one thing, it was all contrary to Pap and Mother's style of religion. They had been brought up in the Campbellite Church, and held that religion was in the head instead of the feet and that there was no truth in those hair-raising religious testimonies. Out at Trinity when they asked all who wanted to go to Heaven to stand up, we sat there just like heathens. And we were too, as far as their religion was concerned. But it was a lot of fun to watch what went on at Trinity, and we went as often as our folks would let us.

the district school

Our schoolhouse was nearly two miles from Old Orchard Farm, but during good weather we shaved off nearly half a mile by taking a short-cut through the fields. We always had to walk to school and back home again unless a big rain came up in the late afternoon. Then some of the folks would come after us in the big wagon so we used to wish hard that it would rain and we would get to ride home. Every once in a while it happened, too.

Pap or one of the older boys would come driving up just as school was out, with a heavy wrap of some kind for each of us. The harder it rained, the better we liked it. We enjoyed huddling under blankets while the wagon sloshed along through the mud and water. All the neighbor kids who could possibly hang on would clamber onto the sides of the wagon and ride, and we let them off in front of their homes.

Sometimes one of the horses would step in a water hole in the road and squash up a great stream of muddy water that would splash all over the kids hanging on the sides. They would set up a yell and we all would laugh.

One time Frank came after us in the wagon when there had been a regular sockdolager of a rain, so that water was running everywhere and the big creek was out of its banks. When we drove up to the wooden bridge south of our house about forty rods, the whole lake bed was covered with water. An area about a hundred yards wide was all cluttered up with driftwood, fence rails, and limbs of trees. The water stood across the road and over the floor of the bridge.

Frank rolled up his britches and waded out to where the bridge ought to be, but it was gone. The black water was all over the place, running like a scared cat. There wasn't anything to do but sit there until the water ran down, so that's just what we did. We spent a couple of hours throwing sticks into the flood, wading along the edge, and petting the horses. Then Frank pulled down a panel of rail fence and drove into the pasture below the road, declaring that he was going to ford the creek down there. The water had gone down a good deal by then and it looked reasonably safe.

It was a ticklish job to drive into that creek. For fifty feet or so the horses waded through slick mud where the water had been over the banks, and then they plunged up to their ears into the main creek. Old Pete and Fox heaved and floundered. Their heads came up about the same time and they turned to head upstream. The wagon swung around into the swift channel and went down just like it was loaded with rocks. It was a good thing there were several of us along for our weight kept the wagon box from floating off. We stood up, waist deep in water, while the horses struggled to get a foothold on the bank. It sure was an exciting moment.

Frank couldn't swim and neither could any of the others except me, and I would have been lucky to have gotten out of there alone without trying to help anybody else. The girls were scared and they commenced to whimper and cry and ended up with screams that made things look worse than ever. We saw Pap running down toward us from the barn, with a pitchfork in his hand. Pap never could run very fast and before he reached us the horses got their feet planted on the bank. In a minute we were all safe and sound.

We had two months of school in the spring, two in the fall, and three in the winter. The schoolhouse was a one-room building, with the girls seated on one side and the boys on the other. There generally were about thirty or forty of us and the course of study took in about everything from the alphabet up to the fifth reader. The classes would be called up to the front seats to recite. A slate blackboard ran all across the end, and there were several maps and a timetable for recitations. It was a poor place for studying, with recitations, shuffling feet, coughing, sneezing, passing water, or the hiccoughs, going most of the time. How we ever managed to learn anything under such circumstances was a question.

All our school teachers in those times were menfolks, as far as I ever heard. My first schoolmaster, a Mr. Huggins, must have been seventy-five years old when he started teaching our school. He stayed with us for five or six years.

He was as clean as a pin and used to take his penknife and scrape out under his fingernails several times a day. One of his thumbnails had been smashed and was all roughed up and two or three times thicker than it ought to be. He used to spend considerable time whittling at it, but he never did get it down to the right size. His hair was as white as snow and he had a long white beard. Huggins had a full mouth of false teeth — the first we ever saw. They shone like the enamel on a coffee cup. He had a habit of kinda prying the lower plate loose with his tongue like he was fishing for something underneath. He had a way too, of munching at something most of the time when he wasn't very busy, but we never found out what it was.

Huggins always wore a pair of carpet slippers at school, and could creep around amongst the seats without making any more noise than a cat. Once in a while he would find some boy in some kind of devilment. Then the culprit had to stay after school was out, with no company but "Ploudin" Huggins, and maybe a dozen of the hardest problems in arithmetic to work out as a penalty.

He always wore a kind of knitted blouse, something like a sweater, but it had buttons up the front and a pocket on each side. He carried his barlow knife, wallet, spectacle case, and three or four pencils in those pockets. Their weight caused the front to sag away down, so that it was several inches longer in front than behind. And as the back got shorter the front kept getting longer 'til it got to be a funny looking garment. He always carried around what he called a "ferrule" in his hand, and a lead pencil stuck behind his ear.

Generally about the middle of the period between taking-up time and the first recess, Old Ploudin would fall asleep in his chair. He had a bad case of palsy, and his little white hands always shook when he was sitting still. When he was awake or busy about something he could keep them fairly quiet, but when he dropped off to sleep he shook a lot worse. Soon the ferrule would drop out of his hand and whack on the floor, and he would jump and come awake. He would slyly reach down and get his ferrule, and try to make out that he hadn't been asleep at all.

But in five minutes he would be dozing again. When he finally got to going strong the pencil would slide down from behind his ear and I have seen him shake off his nose glasses. He snored, too. Between the snores and dropping pencils, there wasn't an ounce of study left in us.

Ploudin Huggins was an unusual teacher. He claimed to have earned a Master's degree and to have taught in Nebraska, Texas, and other states, but his thirty dollar a month salary was an average one for Iowa in those days. I learned the alphabet from him, as well as my addition, subtraction, multiplication and division.

Above all else, however, we learned good manners from Huggins. He was a stickler for teaching courtesy in everything, such as always letting the other scholars drink out of the dipper first. He was the only teacher we ever heard of who put such emphasis upon courtesy and manners. Frequently he lined us up on the front bench to have us repeat in unison, "Papa, potatoes, poultry, prunes, and prisms." Again and again we repeated those words. They shaped our mouths properly, Huggins claimed. Years later I discovered this routine in one of Charles Dickens' novels.

We often carried apples to school with us to nibble on during "books." It was a simple thing to slip one out, take a quick bite, and shove it under the desk cover without being detected. We had to eat the cores and seeds, however, to prevent the schoolmaster from finding any evidence of our forbidden fruit. But we found that we could eat the apple cores if we had to, and the seeds didn't taste too bad after we got used to them.

Every scholar in the school liked to go after a fresh

bucket of water. The water bucket always sat on a wooden bench by the front door. A single tin dipper hung next to it and everybody except the teacher drank out of it. He had a little pewter cup, not much bigger than a good sized thimble, which he carefully wiped with his handkerchief before putting away. As often as forty times a day some student would hold up his hand, snap his fingers, and ask: "Kin I get a drink of water?" Nearly always the teacher would nod and the scholar would go tripping up to the bucket and take a sip or two, and pour the rest back in the bucket. He didn't really want a drink. It was just another way of changing from one thing to another, for we got restless shut up in one room too long.

Sometime between noon and the last recess it was the rule that somebody could fetch a bucket of water. The teacher would walk back and take a look in the bucket, and if there wasn't much more than a dipperful or two, he would nod at the boy that he could go. The boy would choose a partner and light out for either Bomboy's or Old Tom Darbyshire's, each house about forty rods away in different directions.

We usually liked to go to the Darbyshire well for water, for if Old Tom were around at the time we would get to hear him "By Goll" something. Generally the water carriers took up a half hour anyway, putting in as much time as they could. At the end they would bounce into the schoolhouse with quite a spurt to let on that they had hurried.

Right away some girl would ask to pass the water,

and make the whole round of the scholars. But she didn't take a separate trip for each dipperful. They all made it go as far as it would, and sometimes as many as five or six would get a swig before it ran dry.

One time the Buchanan boys brought a half dozen percussion caps that were used to make shotguns go off. They placed them on a flat rock and smashed them with another rock. Each one popped most as loud as a firecracker. But pretty soon the teacher heard the noise and came right out and put a stop to it. We just went off down the road a ways, out of hearing, and finished up the rest of the caps. It was great sport for all us youngsters, for the Buchanan boys claimed you had to do it just right or get your head blown off.

The next day three other boys brought some caps, and before a week went by there wasn't a gun cap left in the school district. I searched all around our house before I found any, but finally did run across some in Joe's box up in his bedroom. They were made for a musket and were three times as big as the ones the other kids had furnished. But I was awfully stingy with them and made them last three weeks.

Ploudin Huggins' health began to fail when he was around eighty-two, and he had to quit teaching school. Our directors hired another man right away by the name of Shenahan — David E. Shenahan. He was a short, stocky man with black chin whiskers, and only one good eye. But we found out in a hurry that he could see more with one eye than most people could with both.

We started in by not liking him a bit, for he was so

awfully different from Ploudin Huggins. But we wound up admiring him more than anybody we knew. He was what the directors called a *disciplinarian,* and they hit the nail right on the head. He had the scholars under his thumb right from the start.

He was the best educated man that our neighborhood ever had. In the six or seven years that he taught our school, we never could think up a question that he couldn't answer right off the bat. Of course, we had no way of telling whether his answers were right, but we always believed they were. He could write a beautiful hand, too.

He wasn't bothered with the modern notion that ornery kids at school shouldn't be whipped. Instead, he seemed to think it was necessary as food and sleep. He called it corporal punishment. At first we didn't understand what that word meant, but many of us soon found out. He always carried a ruler in his hand, and he knew how to use it. It was a dull day at our school when he didn't whip a half dozen kids for some devilment.

He would slip up behind a lazy boy lolling over a book and not looking at it a bit, cuff him over the scalp, and wake him up to his studies. He called the worst cases right out in front to dress them down. Big and little, boys and girls, all fared alike. He would have made a wonderful carpet beater.

But we learned fast under David E. Shenahan. The directors used to come on Friday afternoons to hear us recite. Finally a good many parents got to coming, too. It was the talk of the district how we learned.

Oral drills were great hobbies with Shenahan. It was the quickest and surest way of getting learning to stick in our heads. At one time I could name all the rivers in the world, tell where they started, and what they emptied into. I knew the rest of geography just like that. I learned all about syntax up to rule nineteen, and could parse nearly anything that was ever written down.

In arithmetic we started in with aliquot parts where Huggins left us, and went through greatest common divisor, least common multiple, cancellation, and then right into fractions, partial payments, simple and compound proportion, and finally all those problems in the back part of Ray's *Third Part Arithmetic*. We even mastered this one: "If the velocity of sound be 1,142 feet per second, and the number of pulsations in a person twenty per minute, what is the distance of a cloud if 20 pulsations be counted between seeing a flash of lightning and hearing the thunder?"

Dennis Bowman was our prize scholar. His pap sent him off to the Academy at Mount Pleasant, where he disappeared and was never heard from again. Some thought he was kidnaped, and some believed he fell in an old well. Anyway, we never got anywhere in a wide and anxious search.

Adolph Overman and Moritz Fisher were both good at reading lessons, but they were better known for their fighting. These two had many fist fights and most of the time had black eyes and red noses.

The first girl I ever took a liking for went to our school. She was pretty as a picture and it made me feel good just to have her dress brush against me as she moved down the aisle at school. We got to passing each other notes in school time, but Shenahan got onto it and put a stop to the practice. He whipped us both at the same time, right before the whole school. A little later I put up a "segar" box on our line fence and used that for a post office. I started it with a letter and she came and got it. Then she mailed one and I went and got it. I used to hide behind the straw stack and watch her come for her letter, and my heart would thump like everything.

But I soon lost her. Jodie Williams, an orphan making his home with us at the time, put a dead cat in our private mail box with a paper tied to its tail. He wrote as near like my writing as he could, "I used to think of you as a sick kitten, and now look!" And he signed my name to it. She put it back in the segar box and never spoke to me again.

Shenahan finally married Jane Darbyshire, a daughter of Old Tom "By Goll." He had boarded there all the time he was our teacher. The wedding was a surprise to everybody. A short time after that he got a job on the *Burlington Hawkeye* and moved away, and we lost the knowingest, fastest, most tireless, painstaking, thorough, and all around first-class school teacher we ever had.

We had some wonderful exhibitions at the end of the winter term. Weeks of time were spent getting it ready. Then when the time came we would build a regular stage, just like a theater, with curtains and everything, and make false faces and costumes for the main parts. We always held these exhibitions at night and brought coal oil lamps and tallow candles to put up around the stage so you could see the performers. Everybody in the district would be there, packed in that little house like sardines, and each one strained his neck to see when his kids came out to perform.

Generally we started with Allen Lee playing a piece on his fiddle. He played all the old tunes like "Jenny Get Your Dumplings Done;" "The Arkansas Traveler;" "Gray Eagle;" "The Irish Washerwoman." He had a way of putting in some extra frills that sure could make the fiddle talk.

Then the curtain would be slid back and Amanda Bowman would come out and speak a piece about maybe, "O where, O where is the sailor man who sailed the wintry sea," and for ten or twelve verses recite the sad story of winter storms, shipwreck, broken hearts, and a lot of sad stuff. Then the twin Harcourt girls would speak a piece in what the teacher called "unison," dressed exactly alike, and looking as much alike as two peas. Their piece was "Lochinvar," and since their lips moved right together and they waved their hands alike, pretty soon you began to think there was only one girl up there.

Then came the school paper with a lot of neighborhood news, all made out of whole cloth. It made some of the folks squirm in places. Lots of folks couldn't keep from laughing right out loud.

The school play was the main thing on the program.

One year we gave "The Country Cousin." Another year it was "The World Against Her." Then there was "Her Grandmother's Ghost," the best thing we ever tried. Our home folks liked it so well that we decided to repeat it at White Cloud schoolhouse, two miles to the west, and charge ten cents to see it, children in arms free.

The directors at White Cloud allowed us to have the use of the schoolhouse if we would furnish our own lamps and pay for the firewood we used. That seemed reasonable enough so we fixed a pasteboard announcement and tacked it on the schoolhouse door. When the evening came for the play we hauled all our traps out there in a big wagon and were all dressed up and ready as much as two hours ahead of time. We waited there 'til nine o'clock before we gave up and went home. The only person who showed up was one of the directors who came to collect for the wood we burned. It was only two bits and some of the big boys in the play chipped in and paid it.

When we asked the director why he thought the folks failed to show up, he allowed that if it had been their own kids giving the play they would have been there, but that they were not much interested in what other kids could do. That put an end to our plans to go on the road with our show, and we felt lucky that we hadn't gone very far from home the first try.

We both hated and loved that district school. We cursed it and praised it. We starved and mistreated it. We thought of it as a necessary evil that had to be endured, and never half appreciated what it did for us.

That school stirred our intellects, exercised our youthful imagination, taught us how to find out things for ourselves, and forced real knowledge into our heads.

I hope that nobody ever tears down that old Darbyshire schoolhouse. I wish it could be kept painted and preserved as long as any of us live who wriggled through a day at that wonderful school. To us, it was a whole lot more than a school — it was a university.

the

singing

professor

Pap was especially fond of music. He bought the first reed organ in our community and youngsters from all around used to come in to sing with the organ. Sister Lida June was our organist. She "picked it up" herself, and could play almost any tune. But for us to sing by, she generally played just chords. We sang mostly church songs, for the only book we had with songs in it was a hymnal. We soon got to be pretty good at it. Inside of a year or so, we had a regular choir at Sunday School.

One day a singing teacher came along, announcing he was going to open a singing school at Yarmouth. He offered to give ten lessons for a dollar. We were all crazy to go. Pap asked the singing teacher if he would take three of us for two dollars, and he said yes, that that was his wholesale price. So Belle, Lida June, and I got to go to the singing school.

There we got our first insight into the mysteries of music. We learned about the staff, the five lines and four spaces, and the added lines above and below. We learned about the signature, sharps and flats, whole notes, half notes, quarter notes, rests, the meaning of *F* and *FF*, *P* and *PP*. We learned the meaning of rythmics, melodics, and dynamics, which had something to do with the pitch of tone, the length of tone, and the power and quality of tone, but I don't remember now which was which.

But mostly we learned to sing some wonderful songs. At the end of the ten nights of singing school, the professor staged a big concert. The twenty-five cent admission fee cleaned up more money than he had taken in for teaching. But it was worth more than it cost to get into our heads and hearts the "rudiments," as he called it, of a musical education. In my case that was all I ever got, but I think yet that it was pretty nifty stuff. I have asked more than a dozen modern musical folks about rhythmics, melodics, and dynamics, and most of them have only the haziest notion about them. Some of them never heard of such things at all.

One of the songs we learned at that singing school went like this:

Lo, the glad May morn, with her rosy light is breaking,
O'er the hills so lovely and fair,
And the pure young buds, from their dewy sleep awaking,
Mirth and music float on the air.

Chorus:

Then away, away, away; then away, away, away,
And a Maying we will go.
Then away, away, away; then away, away, away,
And a Maying we will go.

There were three verses in all, and by the time we got to the chorus the third time everybody was going full tilt, and we really made it hum. Six or seven of these songs were sung together, and four or five of our crowd were soloists. Since I was not one of the soloists, I liked the other numbers better.

But the prize song of them all, I always thought, was about the "Little Vale With Fairy Meadows," and it started off like this:

Little vale with fairy meadows,
Trees that spread their leafy hands,
Flowers clothed in brightest beauty,
Lovelier far than eastern lands.
Scenes of fondest recollections,
Lovely village of the vale,
Sacred to the soul's reflection,
Little village in the vale.

Then right after we had all sung that in what the professor called "unison," we went into a rousing chorus, and one of the best girl singers started in with an obligato. She used different words and a different tune, but it fitted in without a hitch and made a pleasant melody.

All this happened in the spring of the year. Once during the summer when some of our neighbors gathered at our house on a Sunday afternoon, somebody suggested that we go into the parlor, by the organ, and have the children sing. That suited us and to do the thing up brown, we started in with "Little Vale With Fairy Meadows." Willis Hale was to sing the tenor part, Belle the alto, I was to sing bass, and Lida June was to play the organ and come in on the obligato. But the song was so arranged that the bass didn't start in on the chorus right at the start. The alto part started the song, a little later the tenor joined in, and still further on the bass came in. So I stood beside the organ, waiting for my cue, while the others sang with all their hearts.

Pap got up and came across the room and ordered me to sing. I tried to explain, without disturbing the other singers, that it wasn't my time yet. But I couldn't get him to understand.

"Sing, I tell you," he shouted in my ear. "What you suppose I gave you lessons for?"

I was terribly embarrassed, and so was everybody else. I couldn't think what to say next, but I did stutter out "Wait a minute." But Pap was not the man to wait. He cuffed me over the ears, right there before the whole crowd, and that fixed me so there wasn't a particle of music in me.

It broke up the party as far as singing was concerned.

Later a married sister explained to Pap how it was, but he just let it go and never made any sort of apology. I never quite forgave him for it, either.

One winter the big boys of the neighborhood put on a rousing minstrel show — about the biggest thing that ever happened in our parts. They had Mrs. Pete Schomp send away for the play, then they met at her house to practice. She was the only person in the township who could read music, and she spent two months drilling into the boys' heads the tunes they had to sing.

Women in the school district sewed and worked on costumes. Since the actors were blacked with burnt cork, their lips reddened with analine, and some had wigs made out of sheeps' wool, you couldn't recognize anybody unless you could recognize the voice. One hit of the show was:

I had a noble mother-in-law, and she was dear to me,
Her voice was music to my ear, her smile was sweet to see.
But she is dead, last week she died, and the doctors gave
    no cause,
Some said she talked herself to death, and broke her poor
    old jaws.

There was more to it, some of it not any too good to print. But, outside of two or three, nobody walked out on the show.

Another song was "The Shoes My Daddy Wore." It was a song and dance arrangement Charlie Mason did, 'cause he was the best jig dancer there was. He could dance a good deal better than he could sing, but they said he averaged pretty high, at that.

Just before my daddy died, he called me to his bed,
I knelt down by his side, and this to me he said,
Come take these good old shoes, I cannot wear them more,
I've worn them more than twenty years, on this old Virginia
    shore.

For these am the shoes my daddy wore.
Then watch me what I doos,
With these old plantation shoes,
For these am the shoes my daddy wore.

Then Charlie broke into a buck and wing dance that just made the platform tremble and the dust fly. Then he sang another verse and danced as long as his breath held out.

The minstrel show also featured some trick acts. One was a fire eater. He talked a lot of nonsense, about nothing in particular, and crammed cotton back in his cheeks at the same time. Then he slipped a live coal into his mouth and began to blow out smoke like a bellows. Pretty soon it turned into a blaze and fire spurted out of his mouth for a couple of feet. It was a mighty fine exhibition, but John Cappes worked on that trick five or six weeks before he could do it without singeing his mouth.

Then they had end men and middle men who asked questions and got off a lot of jokes on people. Some of the jokes were pretty good, although a few were a little raw and let out things about folks that they didn't want everybody to know. That caused some talk, but it blew over after a while.

The big show was staged in an old log house that wasn't being lived in at the time. It would seat only thirty, and the show had to be given four times before everybody got to see it. They charged two bits and cleaned up money enough to pay for the play and the three dollars rent on the log house. It sure was a great success in every way.

Mrs. Schomp allowed that the show aroused the people to a better appreciation of art. She probably was right about it, too. She was a wonderful smart woman and they wouldn't have gotten anywhere with that show without her help.

Once in a while a slight-of-hand performer gave an exhibition in our schoolhouse that was pretty fair. Nothing I ever saw though, through all the years of growing up between the Hawkeye Horizons, came anywhere near gunshot of the big minstrel show the boys put on that winter in the little log house by the road. Every time I have sung those songs, they have taken me right back there among those big boys we kids always looked up to, the ones who knew how to smoke and chew tobacco.

yankee

jack

About once every month in the summertime Yankee Jack would come driving by with his huckster wagon. Yankee Jack was a dark complexioned, little dried-up bachelor who didn't have any folks nearer than New Hampshire. He knew everybody in the county and had a good time riding all over, cooking and eating out of doors every day, doing all the time just what we got to do only once in a great while. It helped a good deal to have Yankee Jack come by, for it made life more pleasant for us all.

Yankee Jack's wagon was built like a little house on wheels, with doors in the back and a little cupola in front for him to ride in, covered with a roof to keep off the sun. When a big rain came he would slide back through a trap door into his little store, for he had lines so long that he could drive from there and keep dry.

When he opened the back doors to get out the extracts and groceries, and other things that Mother used to trade chickens for, a pleasant odor came out. There was most everything in that wagon: calico, gingham, shoes, hats, extracts, groceries and a whole lot more. Along the sides he had strung buckets, and on top he carried a lot of coops to hold the chickens he traded for. Under the side he had built an airtight box, with a padlock on it, for carrying butter. Beside his driving seat he had a place for egg cases. Right below where his feet rested on the dashboard he kept his grub, cooking things, and other personal gear.

Yankee Jack always had something to tell us about what was going on in another township, or how a big bridge was washed out, or something like that. He told us once about driving through a swarm of bees which lit all over him, got tangled up in his chicken coops, and bothered him for several days before he got rid of them. Another time he told of driving seven or eight miles over a swarm of traveling potato bugs crossing the road. He claimed they were more than six inches deep in the road and his horses and wagon wheels squashed bushels of them. The bugs made big blisters on the horses' fetlocks and took all the paint off the wagon wheels half way to the hubs, he said.

There was nearly always a big scare going around about a tiger getting away from a circus and running loose in the woods, and lots of people claimed they got a glimpse of him a time or two. Yankee Jack could be depended on to keep us posted on where he was, for he went everywhere and claimed he had seen the tiger several times, right out in the open road.

All in all, he was a mighty interesting person to us. He was a model for many of us boys who wanted to be peddlers like Yankee Jack and see the world for ourselves. As we grew older, we lost interest in Yankee Jack.

About that time a man came through the country peddling a book called *Peele's Popular Educator*, and I wanted one so bad I could hardly stand it. I asked Mother if she could do anything with Pap about buying it for me, and she tried. But Pap said four dollars was not picked up in the road every day, and we knew by that his mind was made up. But Mother patted me on the head and said she would try to help me out.

By the time the man came back in about a week, Mother had sold several pounds of butter and ten or twelve dozen eggs, giving her a dollar and fifty cents. She told the peddler that if he would leave the book she would pay him the balance with egg and butter money within six weeks. But he wouldn't do it and drove off, and I was just heartbroken. Next day was Sunday, and

John Conkling and his family came riding by in their democrat and asked me to go along to Sunday School. On the way to church I told John about the fine book and how bad I felt about not having one. He was mighty interested, and when we got back to our house he called Pap out and told him he ought to get me that book. He said not many boys were as crazy about good books as I was, and while it wasn't any of his business, he told Pap he would like to see me get the book.

Pap gave me a runt pig that evening, and told me if I would doctor it up, feed it well, and make a good shoat out of it, in a few months it would sell for enough to pay for the book. So at it I went, just tickled pink, for it was the first thing Pap had ever given me.

But before two weeks went by my sister Gussie came home on a visit from Morning Sun, where she had been working in brother Bob's millinery store. She offered to lend me the two dollars and fifty cents I was shy, and told me I could pay her back when I sold the pig. The peddler had left his name and post office address on a slip of paper, so I wrote him a letter. He came the day after he got it and delivered the book.

For months after that I didn't do anything else, all my spare time, but study that book. It had everything in it — long measure, dry measure, apothecary weight, troy weight, how to calculate the bushels of corn in a crib and hay in a mow or stack, and goodness knows how many thousands more things. It had pictures of all the flags in the world, the signs of the zodiac, all about eclipses, astronomy, all the presidents, generals, inventors, and "big" men. If there was anything Peele forgot to put in that book, I never found it out. Ask any question you pleased, you could find the answer in *Peele's Popular Educator*.

There were pages of the finest handwriting I had ever seen. The capital letters were all shaded, and at the end of lots of words would be great scrolls, and maybe a good looking bird perched right in one. There was an uncommon fine drawing of an American Eagle, and a picture of the Saviour made with a pen without taking it off the paper. I practiced all these things myself, over and over and over, 'til I got to be the talk of the neighborhood for the fine things I could make with a pen. Other boys worked at the same thing, and that winter we had a writing school at Zion's hall, taught by a fine writer named Burns, who ran the telegraph office.

Peele's Popular Educator opened up a new world for me. When I had learned all I could from it, I managed to get more good books. Mother bought *The Footprints of Time* and *General Grant's Book,* and Chauncey Blodgett let me borrow books to read. I sort of lost all hankering for devilment and studied like a good fellow. Once I got a taste for things like that, I began to feel like somebody.

a yarmouth saturday night

The little town of Yarmouth — where we traded, got our mail and had our blacksmithing done — was a mighty interesting place. After working all alone in the fields, and not seeing anybody but our own folks for several days at a stretch, it was quite a treat to go to Yarmouth and see some new faces.

Yarmouth wasn't much of a town — only three stores

and a few houses. But it was a big improvement over what we had before the narrow gauge railroad was built through. Before that it was ten miles to a railroad track. We got our mail at a post office called La Vega, which was kept by the Lotspietch family in their own farmhouse, nearly four miles away.

But Yarmouth built right up, with a boom, as soon as the depot was finished, and in a year or two was big as it ever got. Since then it has gotten smaller, if anything.

A good many boys in our neighborhood went to Yarmouth about every Saturday afternoon and had a regular picnic of a time all afternoon. They would go back home to do the night chores and eat supper, and then go right back to town to spend the evening. Pap never let us go in the daytime, unless it was too wet to work in the fields — and even then he generally could find weeds for us to cut, or hedge to trim, or fence to fix. But we always got to go on Saturday nights, and we were mighty glad of that.

As many as forty or fifty teams would be tied in rows all along the hitchracks, and the streets would be just swarming with folks. Nearly everybody would be there, and sometimes people came from as far off as six or seven miles. In every store people would be sitting around on sugar sacks, nail kegs, and right on the counters — talking about the weather, and the crops, and other interesting things. Dave Michaels always had a lot of funny stories to tell, and some of them were pretty nippy for a young person to hear. At the end nearly everybody would break out in a hearty laugh, and nod at one another and wink.

In Andy Cline's store, back toward the stove, there would be two fellows bent over a checker board and six or eight others standing around looking on. Every little bit one of the spectators would ask why the players didn't move this man and take two, or something like that. Andy was one of the best checker players in the county, I reckon, and his two boys had to do the waiting on customers whenever anybody bantered him for a game. John Conkling was stiff competition, and James Robert Hale had to be watched pretty close, for he had a checker book and studied it 'til he knew nearly every move on the board. All the good players kind of went in "cahoots" against James Robert, and would move so as not to let him get the men in the shape he wanted them, or it was bound to be his game. Every Saturday night, and all day long when there was a big rain, they were right at it, tooth and nail.

We would go over to Ben Ward's shack, where he had lemonade, peanuts, candy, and ice cream for sale. He also had a little pool table, and cigars, tobacco, and a cigar box full of pipe tobacco on the counter, free to all. It was a good smelling place — pleasant to be in whether you bought anything or not, and Old Ben generally had a new story or two to tell. It was the general opinion that he held it over Dave Michaels a little when it came to stories.

For the most part we boys had our good times out of doors, even at Yarmouth. We played every kind of a game you ever heard of. We wrestled, jumped, ran foot races, pulled square holts, chinned, boxed hats, threw the fifty-pound test weight, and worked ourselves up into a regular lather. If we had been forced to work half that hard on the farm, we would have nearly died, I'm sure. We kept it up as late as ten o'clock sometimes, and we were always sorry when the stores closed and we had to go home.

Over at the Henry County Fair at Mt. Pleasant, I got to see two real cowboys from the "wild and woolly West." They were all dressed up in leather britches, red flannel shirts, and broad brimmed hats. They rode into the ring on sure enough broncos, their saddles had double cinches, big stirrups, and a horn a foot high, spurs dangled from high top boots, and strings of buckskin hung down from their horses' bits. The sight nearly set me wild.

The cowboys took after a little herd of wild horses that had been brought there from the West. After a good deal of galloping and circling around, they roped one of them and threw him down so hard we thought it surely had broken his neck. The two got off, blindfolded the horse and let him up, strapped a saddle on his back, and forced a riding bridle on him. Then one cowboy got on and away went the wild pony, bucking, pitching, sunfishing, and twisting this way and that — and that wonderful cowboy just sat there in the saddle as comfortable as tho it was a rocking chair. After a while the pony got winded and stopped cavorting around. The cowboy jumped off and bowed at the crowd, and everybody waved handkerchiefs and yelled and clapped for five minutes. Right then I decided to be a cowboy.

On the way home I thought up what I was going to do. And the first idle time I had, I brought a three-year-old mule out of the pasture. It had never had even a halter on. I locked him behind a rail in a box stall in the barn, then strapped a sheepskin on his back, put a blind bridle on him, and got aboard. I kicked the rail loose and that big colt went out of the barn sidewise in the biggest kind of a hurry. He knocked several boards off. He backed right through a high picket fence. Then he commenced to buck and pitch something awful, but I stuck on by holding the strap that held the sheepskin. Next he ran under an apple tree and nearly scraped the top of my head off, as I scootched down trying my best to miss the limb. He went through a hedge and into the potato patch and was going through the wickedest kind of maneuvers when I dropped off. It took some time to pick all the dirt out of my right ear, my neck was all twisted around to one side, and I was as dizzy as could be for a day or so.

I never tried being a cowboy again. I know now that being tuckered out that easy was a sure sign that I wasn't ever cut out for a cowboy anyhow.

Then I got a notion that I wanted to be a clown. I had seen some good ones at a circus, noticed how everybody laughed at their antics, and just itched to have them laugh at me in the same way. It was a tedious business to work up to, but I set to work as soon as I found time. I rigged up a springboard by using a bridge plank stuck under the water trough, and held up by a chunk of wood. I got so I could jump off of this and turn a somersault and light on a straw tick and keep my feet. Then I trained two old tame cows we had to stand side by side in front of my springboard while I made the leap and somersaulted over their backs. It took a long time to train them to stand still, but at last they gave in, and generally stayed right there 'til I lit on the tick.

One Saturday afternoon I decided to give a matinee performance and invited my sister to see my act. I got hold of a Mother Hubbard dress belonging to one of the girls, painted my face with flour, and wore a paper hat running up to a high peak. The hat had been used in one of the schoolhouse plays the winter before. When I had everything ready, I opened the back barn door and my sisters stood up there while I climbed my springboard to show off.

I came down the board as fast as I could run — that Mother Hubbard flapping in the breeze — and made a try at a somersault. But the old cows were not used to the suit I had on and started to run away. Being upside down in the air at the time, I didn't know they were moving, and I came down astraddle of one's neck, right over its horns. They were gentle enough cows and of course wouldn't hook anybody, but in scrambling off those horns I lost a big piece out of the Mother Hubbard dress. One old cow carried it around several days.

When I lit, the girls busted out laughing, and then came running down to see if I had been killed. They put linament on me several places, and Pap took several stitches with a rowel, sewing up a gash in my leg. A day or two later I had a high fever, and thought I was going to die before I got over it. I guess I must have been a quitter, because I never tried the clown business after that, and I made a pretty good hand in the field for a long time. Just settled right down, Pap said.

Another time I got the prize fighting craze. The *Police Gazette* was covered with colored pictures of John L. Sullivan and Jake Kilrain, and an article about their seventy-round fight at New Orleans covered three or four pages. I had never read anything that stirred me up like that did, and went to work right away to learn to be a prize fighter. I pulled wool off the fences, where the sheep had scraped under, and sewed it on the back of Pap's mittens for stuffing. It made tolerably good boxing gloves, too. I got a good many boys to practice with me, and since I was bigger than most of them, I got along fine.

One day I put the gloves on with a big fellow from New London who was out our way with his father, a cattle buyer, and that ended all the notion I ever had to be a prize fighter. He was one of the most discouraging fellows I ever knew. He thumped me right on the head, the mouth, and the nose just as many times as he liked. There wasn't any way I could find to prevent it. Pretty soon my nose was bleeding, one eye was about swollen shut, and I had a kind of sick feeling inside.

At the end of the third round my seconds threw a towel in the air, which was the signal that the fight was over as far as I was concerned. I don't mind saying that I was glad they did. I could see more stars than you can see on a clear night in the dark of the moon, and had some queer feeling inside that I can't describe. Just like all my other ventures, this crazy notion I had about being a gladiator bogged down — like a cow in the mud — right there. I never tried it again and gave my sheepskin boxing gloves to a couple of girls that lived neighbors to us. They made a chair cushion out of them for their grandpa, so they were put to some good use after all.

I grew to be a good deal interested in girls, and finally the hankering broke out on me thick as chicken pox. All the things I had learned helped out more than you would think in getting along with girls. There wasn't a boy in our neighborhood who could hold a candle to me at writing a fine hand. I made a good many drawings of birds sitting on nests, all surrounded with the finest kind of scroll work, with maybe down below a pennant dangling with a girl's name printed on it. I never saw a girl who didn't take to that kind of present.

Then I had it over most of the boys in things to talk about. Riding around nights, I could pick out different stars and tell the girls their names, and how far off they were. I knew how to figure how many turns a buggy wheel made in going a mile. I knew a good deal about wild plants, and specific gravity, and induction, and could recite poetry from several books.

It got Belle Johnson's papa more interested in me than Belle was. He was a smart man, well read, and liked to talk to me so well that when I went there to see his pretty daughter, he took up most of the time himself talking things over with me. Belle was a luscious, red lipped, beautiful girl, and I fell in love with her just the worst way. But I never got very far with it. She wasn't any older, but she seemed older than I was, and she got interested in an older fellow who had a top buggy of his own, so she kind of drifted away from me.

When the time came just right, it was all settled for me in a few minutes. When I met my Lucy at choir practice, she looked just like I had always wanted my best girl to look. When we were introduced, we shook hands across the top of the organ, and Ellen Hale was playing a church tune about, "Happy Day That Fixed My Choice." In the light of what happened afterwards, it seemed almost like a good omen. Organ notes never joined in making any better melody than we did right from the start, and it has always been that way.

Pap's trying to bust up that match a year or two later just fastened it down tighter, and the time came when I stopped riding horseback fifteen miles every Sunday to see her, and just went down and got her, and have had her ever since.

But back of it all stand a lot of wonderful experiences — experiences that nobody can get unless he is lucky enough to be born and brought up in the open country. Most of those experiences are as clear as though they happened only a year or so ago. I like to call them up and enjoy them over again.

One of the brightest and sweetest recollections is the

picture of Mother, the busy little woman who never thought of herself in her life, but just put her time in being lovely to everybody she ever met. And there is Pap, too — hard to understand and impossible to manage, but when you came to find him out, a likable, heroic, clean and wonderful man that any boy ought to be proud to have for a father.